ARCHITECTURE LIVE PROJECTS

Architecture Live Projects provides a persuasive, evidence-based advocacy for moving a particular kind of architectural learning, known as Live Projects, towards a holistic integration into current and future architectural curricula.

Live Projects are work completed in the borderlands between architectural education and built environment practice; they include design/build work, community-based design, urban advocacy consulting and a host of other forms and models described by the book's international group of authors. Because of their position, Live Projects as a vehicle for simultaneously providing teaching and service has the potential to recalibrate the contesting claims that both academia and profession make on architecture.

This collection of essays and case studies consolidates current discussions on theory and learning ambitions, academic best practices, negotiation with licensure and accreditation, and considerations of architectural integrity. It is an invaluable resource for current and future Live Projects advocates – whether they aim to move from pedagogy into practice or practice into pedagogy.

Harriet Harriss is a chartered architect and a senior lecturer in Architecture at Oxford Brookes University, and the founding director of Live Lab: a university situated incubator for architecture business start-ups committed to social innovation. Harriet's teaching and research publications explore how architects can enable people to live better lives and how the public or 'end users' can be given a more active role in shaping the spaces and communities in which they live and work.

Lynnette Widder teaches at Columbia University and practises architectural design with aardvarchitecture in New York. From 2006 to 2012, she was Head of the Department of Architecture at the Rhode Island School of Design, and from 1994 to 1998 was an editor of the bilingual quarterly *Daidalos*. She coauthored *Ira Rakatansky: As Modern as Tomorrow* (2010).

ARCHITECTURE LIVE PROJECTS

Pedagogy into practice

Edited by Harriet Harriss and Lynnette Widder

Routledge
Taylor & Francis Group

LONDON AND NEW YORK

First edition published 2014
by Routledge
2 Park Square, Milton Park, Abingdon, Oxon OX14 4RN

Simultaneously published in the USA and Canada
by Routledge
711 Third Avenue, New York, NY 10017

Routledge is an imprint of the Taylor & Francis Group, an informa
business

British Library Cataloguing in Publication Data
A catalogue record for this book is available from the British Library

Library of Congress Cataloging in Publication Data
Architecture Live Projects : pedagogy into practice / [edited by]
Harriet Harriss & Lynnette Widder. – First edition.
    pages cm
    Includes bibliographical references and index.
    1. Architecture–Study and teaching (Higher)
    2. Architects–Training of.
    I. Harriss, Harriet, editor of compilation. II. Widder, Lynnette,
    editor of compilation.
NA2005.A69 2014   720.92–dc23
2013040773

ISBN: 978-0-415-73361-8 (hbk)
ISBN: 978-0-415-73352-6 (pbk)
ISBN: 978-1-315-78076-4 (ebk)

Typeset in Bembo
by Sunrise Setting Ltd, Paignton, UK

Printed and bound in Great Britain by
TJ International Ltd, Padstow, Cornwall

Dedicated to Huxley, Curvier, Rudyard, Carlos, Freya, Yewbert, Atticus, Thilo, Skoukje and Unicorn

CONTENTS

FIGURES

CONTRIBUTORS

Jane Anderson is co-founder of the online Live Projects Network and also OB1 LIVE, a programme of Live Projects at Oxford Brookes School of Architecture, where she leads the undergraduate architecture programme.

Barnaby Bennett is currently completing his PhD on the relationship between temporary architecture and the public in post-quake Christchurch at UTS, Sydney, and is director and founder of the publishing cooperative Freerange Press.

James Benedict Brown is a Lecturer in Architecture at Norwich University of the Arts. His PhD, which developed a pedagogical critique of the Live Project, was completed in 2012 at Queen's University Belfast.

Alan Chandler is a Specialist Conservation Architect and founding partner of the practice Arts Lettres Techniques and is Research Leader for Architecture and the Built Environment at the University of East London.

Prue Chiles is an academic in the School of Architecture at the University of Sheffield and is a founding partner of Co-Arch Studio, formerly Prue Chiles Architects. She initiated the Live Project programme at Sheffield in 1998.

Megan Clark is Program Manager for ENGAGE at CCA and Manager of Strategic Partnerships for the Center for Art & Public Life at California College of the Arts in Oakland, California.

Sofia Davies is an Oxford Brookes graduate who specialized in Development and Emergency Practice as part of her Diploma in Architecture. She currently works in a small architecture practice in London.

Mel Dodd is a founding partner and collaborator at MUF Architects and directs the Spatial Practices course at Central St Martins in London.

Charlie Fisher is a former student of the Masters in Architecture, Development and Emergency Practice at Oxford Brookes University and is currently involved in an open-source Architecture and a WikiHouse research and development initiative.

Daisy Froud is a founder of architecture practice AOC, where she leads their brief-building and participatory design work. She is a Tutor and Lecturer in History and Theory on the MArch programme at the Bartlett School of Architecture, London.

David Gloster is Director of Education at the RIBA, and has taught and practised architecture in the UK for over 30 years.

Nils Gore is an Associate Professor in Architecture at the University of Kansas (KU), where he engages students in Live Project learning. He is also a licensed architect.

Harriet Harriss (RIBA, FRSA, FHEA) is a Senior Lecturer in Architecture at Oxford Brookes University, a Higher Education Academy Internationalization Awardee and Fellow, and the founding director of Live Lab, an award-winning social innovation start-up incubator for graduate architecture students.

Michael Hughes is a partner in the architecture firm Catovic Hughes Design, Director of the Tectonic Landscapes Design–Build Initiative and Head of the Department of Architecture at the American University of Sharjah in the United Arab Emirates.

Christopher Livingston is an Associate Professor with the School of Architecture at Montana State University, Bozeman, MT, where he teaches design studies and building construction courses.

Natasha Lofthouse is a former student of the Masters in Architecture, Development and Emergency Practice at Oxford Brookes University and works as an architectural assistant at Fluid Architects in London.

Alex MacLaren is a partner in Wyatt MacLaren Architects and a trustee of Teambuild Association. She also leads an undergraduate Design Studio at the University of Edinburgh.

Anne Markey (BArch, MSc(Arch), RIBA) is Head of Projects, CPD and Enterprise at the Sir John Cass Faculty of Art, Architecture and Design, London Metropolitan University. She has over 20 years' experience as an architect in private practice and is also a director of Phelan Architects, a practice that she founded in 2009 with her partner Brendan Phelan.

Sebastian Messer is a Chartered Architect and Senior Lecturer in Architecture at Northumbria University as well as co-founder of the GRAD Programme.

Ruth Morrow is Professor of Architecture at Queen's University Belfast, curatorial adviser to the PS2 art collective in Belfast and Director of Tactility Factory.

Frank Mruk (AIA, RIBA) is the Associate Dean at New York Institute of Technology's School of Architecture and Design and a past co-director of the Masters in Urban and Regional Design programme. He is also a founding partner of DMA Architects and executive director of the New York Center for Strategic Innovation.

Shauntel Nelson graduated in 2012 with a Master of Architecture from Montana State University and is currently working for Williams & Associates Architects in Spearfish, South Dakota.

Colin Priest is Course Leader for BA(Hons) Interior and Spatial Design at Chelsea College of Art and Design and founder of Studio Columba.

Ryan Reynolds is a Lecturer in Theatre and Film Studies at the University of Canterbury in Christchurch, New Zealand, and long-standing collaborator with experimental troupe Free Theatre Christchurch. After the 2010 earthquakes he co-founded and now chairs the Gap Filler Trust, which activates vacant sites throughout the city with temporary creative projects for public benefit.

Beverly A. Sandalack is founder of the Urban Lab and Professor and Associate Dean (Academic) in the Faculty of Environmental Design at the University of Calgary. She is a registered landscape architect and planner.

Christine Theodoropoulos is an architect and engineer, and Dean of the College of Architecture and Environmental Design at the California Polytechnic State University, San Luis Obispo. At Cal Poly she leads programmes in architecture, landscape architecture, architectural engineering and planning, and chairs visiting teams for the National Architectural Accrediting Board (NAAB).

Christian Volkmann is an Associate Professor at the Spitzer School of Architecture, City College of New York. He has developed several pedagogic concepts focusing on the integration of technical and environmental topics into the design process and the interrelated task of design–build implementation.

Simon Warren is a co-founder of the Project Office and course leader for the Master of Architecture at Leeds Metropolitan University.

Lynnette Widder serves on the full-faculty in Sustainability Management at Columbia University in New York. She is also partner in the architecture firm aardvarchitecture.

Bruce Wrightsman is an Assistant Professor of Architecture at Kansas State University in Manhattan, Kansas.

Mimi Zeiger is a Los Angeles-based journalist and critic covering architecture and art. She has lectured internationally on the Interventionist Toolkit, a series of articles on alternative urbanist practice she wrote for *Places Journal*.

Alfred Zollinger currently directs the Design Workshop, Parsons design and build programme, and is a co-principal of Matter Practice, an architecture and exhibition-design firm in Brooklyn, NYC.

FOREWORD

Live Project love: building a framework for Live Projects

Ruth Morrow

Introduction

Live Projects exist between the two tectonic plates of learning in academia and in practice. This chapter aims to frame Live Projects more clearly in order to encapsulate, critique, progress, and elevate the work. Ultimately it aims to share the Live Project love. It draws on a range of current publications on Live Projects, in particular papers presented at the International Symposium, *Architecture 'Live Projects' Pedagogy*, in May 2012[1] and the author's own teaching experience.[2] But, while the breadth of Live Projects is wide, we still seem unable to locate Live Projects within a pedagogical context, tending instead to limit descriptions and hence analysis to the architectural process and outcome.

There is a need to create an operational and theoretical framework for this mode of pedagogy. It is important to recognize that architectural pedagogy, even in the form of Live Projects, is not architectural practice, though it frequently overlaps. Even though Live Projects may come very close to architectural practice, particularly at postgraduate level, they still remain a pedagogical tool. And while they may be 'live', unpredictable, contingent, and even 'student-led', they are still a pedagogical construct of higher education.

We need an overarching framework that goes beyond collating descriptions of project A, B, or C and, instead, suggests coherent and crafted pedagogies. To build that pedagogical framework around Live Projects we need the component parts of a conceptual framework: a working definition, categorized exemplars, and analysis of content and method, that are specific, though not necessarily exclusive, to the concept.

Working definition and back catalogue

A cursory glance at a selection of definitions for Live Projects shows that this first level of building a framework is relatively evolved. Below are two such definitions: an early and a more recent attempt to encapsulate Live Projects:[3]

The live project is defined here as a type of design project that is distinct from a typical studio project in its engagement of real clients or users, in real-time settings. Students are taken out of the studio setting, and repositioned in the 'real-world'.

(Sara 2004)

A live project comprises the negotiation of a brief, timescale, budget and product between a client and an educational institution.

(Anderson and Priest 2012)

Between these two definitions one sees a development from describing the activity to including the context. Anderson and Priest's definition places the 'educational institution' for the first time into the definition, providing us with the means to sift and sort case studies, beginning a process of classification through which a community and lineage can emerge.

Combining the recent body of work that has emerged from sustained Live Project programmes at UK universities[4] with the vibrant design/build culture that occurs in the US and other countries,[5] we are starting to build a comprehensive catalogue where work can be cross-referenced and patterns identified. The 'Live Projects Network'[6] and, indeed, this publication provide further vehicles to extend the catalogue, reveal characteristics and traits, and allow those involved in architectural education to critically contextualize and develop their own Live Project pedagogies.

Considering content

Most constructed forms of teaching/learning start with the question: What do we want (students) to learn? Live Projects expand that to ask: What more do we want architecture students to learn? Tutors create Live Projects, sometimes instinctively, in response to perceived gaps in education or areas of practice that normative design studios fail to address. Several such areas emerge:

People. Live Projects are used to expose students to a wide variety of people implicated in architectural processes – that is, other professions, contractors, client bodies, and user groups, particularly those outside the architect's normal sphere.[7]

Processes. Live Projects offer students opportunities to participate in stages beyond the design phase: defining briefs, fundraising, costing projects, and developing marketing strategies.

Materials/construction. Design/build Live Projects allow students to directly interact with materials and the process of assembly. They gain not only knowledge but also knowhow[8] that later informs their development and practice as architects.

Other skills. Long lists of skills are identified as emerging from Live Projects. As Live Projects' range has increased, so too has the list of skills that emerge from them. Typically skills noted are group work, audience-responsive communication skills, reporting, and negotiation, but increasingly other skills such as marketing, dealing with contingency, social media promotion, etc. have become part of Live Projects.

Value systems. Live Projects release students from the less-than-transparent values that exist in the design studio.[9] The question of who has the authority to judge architecture, where and when, frequently emerges, though it is rarely resolved.[10] Knowing that there are conflicting and contentious views of architecture is valuable for students as they begin to triangulate their own positions. The value and nature of architectural practice itself also comes under scrutiny in Live Projects. They provide a place from which students can explore 'new ways of practicing architecture and … rethink the traditional role of the architect as a service provider …' (Denicke-Polcher and Khonsari 2012: 3).

Considering method

Whilst the pedagogical content of Live Projects is becoming clearer, the methods used have to be 'extracted' from writings on the subject. At the symposium cited, people talked extensively about why and what, but few outlined how. Fewer still adopted the language of learning intentions, outcomes, assessment means, and criteria. And, while the use of such terminology does not directly imply meaningful learning, we do need to capture and understand its pedagogical methodologies and structures in order to refine them. Three areas emerge initially from the writing on Live Projects:

Support. Those involved in delivering Live Projects naturally evolve systems and processes that support the process over time. They do so not just in regard to students but, significantly, also in support of clients. Support comes in various forms. In some cases, tutors select projects, prepare the ground, and manage the process to varying degrees in order to ensure positive outcomes.[11] In other cases, students select or bring projects themselves, increasing their understanding, ownership, and commitment from the beginning.[12] Handbooks and 'resource and survival packs' are generated (Chiles and Till 2009) and 'Live Project offices' have been established to support Live Projects before, during, and after the process.[13]

Timing. Probably the greatest area of discussion for Live Project practitioners is timing and location in the curriculum. Many argue that design/build projects do not fit easily into semester structures unless heavily choreographed.[14] Some design tutors overcome this disjuncture by straddling semesters.[15] The expectation is that, later in the curriculum, Live Projects become longer, like 'lite' versions of practice. In fact, some argue that Live Projects have no place at undergraduate level. However, if we return to the evolving definition of Live Projects, particularly Anderson and Priest's definition, we see that the institution and, by association, its operational context is part of the Live Project framework. In other words, both higher education and practice make up the context for Live Projects. Creative practitioners of Live Project pedagogy must surely be sufficiently skilled to work within both arenas.

Critique. Given that the 'crit' plays such a central role in the culture of architectural education it is odd that discussion about assessment and critique is noticeably scarce in the writings around Live Projects. Where assessment is discussed, it is in the context of keeping it to a minimum (MacLaren 2012: 7) or looking for opportunities to evaluate outcomes in other areas of the course.[16] In general, assessment and critique feel uncertain and as yet unresolved. Chiles and Till's description of a final Live Projects presentation echoes this uncertainty. These, they say, 'are not critiques but formal presentations run by the student body'. They admit that students still feel that tutors sometimes 'bring more traditional power relationships back into the review' (Chiles and Till 2009: 5). Like at Sheffield and other places, our experience with the one-week 'Street Society' Live Project at Queen's Belfast has led us to assess Live Projects elsewhere in the curriculum. It is purposefully concluded *not* by a crit, but rather by a public celebration.

Perhaps we require a clearer theoretical and practical understanding of the differences between *assessment, valorization* and *critique*, and, more particularly, their role, timing, and significance in developing and sustaining students' creative practice.[17]

Conclusions

Live Projects are increasing in number and sophistication and, with that, the formation of a defining and supporting framework is almost inevitable. There are certainly areas within their content, method, and critique that require further examination, including the nature of the relationship between Design Studio projects and Live Projects. Design Studio provides the perfect risk-free environment to strip away context, conditions, and uncontrollable complexities and allow an abstracted space in which to examine concepts in detail and isolation.

If Live Projects are to take up a different role from that of Design Studio projects, it is because they exist in complex, unpredictable spaces where skills of negotiation, fleetness of foot, resourcefulness, time management, and ability to deliver within (changing) constraints to a range of audiences are at stake and of value. In that case, Live Projects must be assessed in a different way to Design Studio projects. This might naturally lead to the evaluation of different types of learners in different ways at different times in the curriculum and ultimately result in a mark sheet whose profile is in flux! Perhaps one measure of the success of a curriculum that integrates both Live and Design Studio projects is that more people are able to find a valued position in the broad church of architectural education.

There are clear tensions between the tectonic plates straddled by Live Projects, creating attempts at repositioning and occasional ruptures, but there is also a heightened potential for new energies and rich deposits. Nonetheless, we still need to frame, test, and question them in order to share the Live Project love...

Notes

1 The International Symposium *Architecture 'Live Projects' Pedagogy* was held in May 2012 at Oxford Brookes University, UK.

2 Morrow contributed a key-note lecture at the 2012 International Symposium *Architecture 'Live Projects' Pedagogy*, drawing on pedagogy outlined in the following publications: Morrow (2007a; 2007b); Morrow and Brown (2011); Morrow and Brown (2012).

3 Other definitions: Watt and Cottrell (2006) and Chiles and Holder (2008).

4 Under the leadership of Bob Fowles (University of Cardiff) and Bill Pirnie (University of Dundee).

5 Countries represented at the International Symposium at Oxford Brookes included the United States, Indonesia, Canada, Qatar, and India.

6 Live Projects Network, an online resource launched by Oxford Brookes University, UK to connect academics, students, and clients involved in Live Projects. Available online at: www.liveprojectsnetwork.org Accessed January 2014.

7 For example, see Andri Yatmo and Atmodiwirjo (2012).

8 For Judy Wajcman (1991) 'knowhow' is a form of knowledge that is 'visual, even tactile, rather than simply verbal or mathematical'.

9 This issue is well discussed in feminist critiques of architectural education, particularly Dutton (1991).

10 Carless (2012) describes a project where children and primary school teachers, acting as guest critics, assess architecture student design work.

11 Michael Hughes' honest critique (2012) outlines the lengths faculty go to 'artificially curtail' and manage a design/build project into a form of choreographed reality in order to 'increase the likelihood of an on-time project completion'.

12 In 'Street Society', an annual constellation of Live Projects run at Queen's University Belfast, a call for project proposals is announced and then shortlisted by postgraduate students who act as project managers. See Morrow and Brown (2011: 11).

13 For example: the Bureau of Design Research (BDR) in the School of Architecture at the University of Sheffield; ASD Project Office at London Metropolitan University; the Project Office at Portsmouth School of Architecture; and more generally initiatives such as the Science Shop (part of an EU-wide network) at Queen's University Belfast.

14 This point was made in Chandler (2012) and Hughes (2012).

15 Denicke-Polcher and Khonsari (2012) advocate Live Projects that start within the semester structure of a taught course but span into vacation and/or the year out (that is, the year required to satisfy Professional Examination (RIBA/ARB Part 3)).

16 For example: Shechter (2012) describes how a learning log is used to capture and assess students' experiences, particularly in respect to evidence of collaborative skills.

17 Critical feedback tends towards the negative. The term 'valorization' reminds us that one of the most supportive strategies in the development of a clear and distinctive form of creative practice is to remind students (and ourselves) when things are going well.

References

Anderson, J., and Priest, C. (2012). 'Developing a Live Projects Network and Flexible Methodology for Live Projects'. Paper presented at *Architecture 'Live Projects' Pedagogy*, Oxford Brookes University, UK.

Andri Yatmo, Y., and Atmodiwirjo, P. (2012). 'Understanding the Structure of Community and the Nature of Intervention: Lessons Learned from Community Live Projects in a Developing Country'. Paper presented at *Architecture 'Live Projects' Pedagogy*, Oxford Brookes University, UK.

Brown, J. B. (2012a). 'Situated Knowledges: Theorising the Live Project'. Paper presented at *Architecture 'Live Projects' Pedagogy*, Oxford Brookes University, UK.

Brown, J. B. (2012b). 'A Critique of the Live Project', PhD thesis, Queen's University, Belfast, UK.

Carless, T. (2012). 'Open School'. Paper presented at *Architecture 'Live Projects' Pedagogy*, Oxford Brookes University, UK.

Chandler, A. (2012). 'Building is a Verb'. Paper presented at *Architecture 'Live Projects' Pedagogy*, Oxford Brookes University, UK.

Chiles, P., and Holder, A. (2008). 'Live Projects'. Extended abstract paper at the Oxford Conference on Architectural Education, Oxford Brookes University, UK.

Chiles, P., and Till, J. (2009). *Live Projects: An Inspirational Model – The Student Perspective*, The Centre for Education in the Built Environment Case Study. Available online at: http://cebe.cf.ac.uk/learning/casestudies/case_pdf/PrueChiles.pdf Accessed January 2014.

Denicke-Polcher, S., and Khonsari, T. (2012). 'Architecture of Multiple Authorship'. Paper presented at *Architecture 'Live Projects' Pedagogy*, Oxford Brookes University, UK.

Dutton, T. A. (1991). 'The Hidden Curriculum and the Design Studio'. In *Voices in Architectural Education: Cultural Politics and Pedagogy*, ed. T. A. Dutton, Bergin and Garvey.

Hughes, M. (2012). 'Constructing a Contingent Pedagogy at Full Scale'. Paper presented at *Architecture 'Live Projects' Pedagogy*, Oxford Brookes University, UK.

MacLaren, A. J. W. (2012). 'Teambuild: New Formats of Delivery of Learning in Construction'. Paper presented at *Architecture 'Live Projects' Pedagogy*, Oxford Brookes University, UK.

Morrow, R. (2007a). 'Building Clouds Drifting Walls: Architectural Pedagogy'. In *Altering Practices: Feminist Politics and Poetics of Space*, ed. Doina Petrescu, Routledge.

Morrow, R. (2007b). 'Creative Transformations'. In *Design Studio Pedagogy: Horizons for the Future*, ed. Ashraf Salama and Nicolas Wilkinson, The Urban International Press.

Morrow, R. (2012). 'Live Project Love'. Paper presented at *Architecture 'Live Projects' Pedagogy*, Oxford Brookes University, UK.

Morrow, R. and Brown, J. (2011). 'Street Society: A Live Project at Queen's University Belfast'. In *Intercultural Interaction in Architectural Education*, ed. Peter Beacock, Geoffrey Makstutis and Robert Mull, ASD Projects, London Metropolitan University, London.

Morrow, R. and Brown, J. (2012). 'Live Projects as Critical Pedagogies'. In *Designing with People*, ed. Esther Charlesworth, Melanie Dodd and Fiona Harrisson, RMIT Training Pty Ltd.

Sara, R. (2004). 'Between the Studio and the Street: The Role of the Live Project in Architectural Education', PhD thesis, University of Sheffield, UK.

Shechter, S. (2012). 'Co-designing Speaker's Corner'. Paper presented at *Architecture 'Live Projects' Pedagogy*, Oxford Brookes University, UK.

Wajcman, J. (1991). *Feminism Confronts Technology*, Polity.

Watt, K. and Cottrell, D. (2006). 'Grounding the Curriculum: Learning from Live Projects in Architectural Education', *International Journal of Learning* 13: 98.

PREFACE

The rub

Mimi Zeiger

Let's start with Daisy Froud and Alfred Zollinger's 'Pedagogy into Practice or Practice into Pedagogy?' dialogue in this volume. Beginning not at the beginning but *in media res* may seem rather awkward when applied to a preface, the very role of which is to anticipate the content to come without revealing too much – to frame, but not flesh out. With Live Projects, however, we need to start in the middle of things. As their name suggests, Live Projects are oft defined within the architectural discipline by their activity, with their conceptual, theoretical, and pedagogical implications only just spelled out in this volume.

Froud, a member of the London-based firm Agents of Change, where she leads participation and community engagement, describes the friction between theory and practice as an active space of experimentation. She calls this area of productivity a "rub", writing, "[i]t is a means to test theories of democracy, of engagement, of the politics of form, and to think about what theories and propositions start to emerge through the experiences and accumulated evidence."

To describe this confluence of agents and constituents, designers and communities, with the word "rub" – a word that is simultaneously soothing and abrading – is to recognize the challenges of Live Projects. The idiom "therein lies the rub" indicates the difficulty of working in-between – not simply between theory and practice, but also between public and private sectors, and between mainstream and disciplinary cultures. The rub comes from marginalization stemming from opposing arenas. On one side is the alignment of Live Projects to Do-It-Yourself home improvement and the efficiencies of design/build, which undermines their pedagogical power. Architecture culture tends to shy away from DIY didactics and "bottom-up" techniques, since these practices often elude formalist critique with their scale, scope, and off-the-shelf material palette. On the other side is the decidedly aformal "social practice." Stemming from the art world, social practice shares similar techniques and goals with Live Projects, including direct community engagement, a drive toward social good, and the emphasis on the activity (and activism) itself – a transformative experience. Social practice, like Live Projects, is just beginning to be institutionalized, raising difficult questions about acceptance and meaning within culture.

In a *New York Times* article entitled "Outside the Citadel, Social Practice Art is Intended to Nurture," author Randy Kennedy summed up the wellspring of participatory practice that had developed since the Occupy Movement while identifying its deep roots in grassroots organizing and post-studio practice dating back to the 1960s, writing:

> Known primarily as social practice, its practitioners freely blur the lines among object making, performance, political activism, community organizing, environmentalism and investigative journalism, creating a deeply participatory art that often flourishes outside the gallery and museum system. And in so doing, they push an old question – "Why is it art?" – as close to the breaking point as contemporary art ever has.
>
> *(Kennedy 2013)*

Which raises an equally old question of Live Projects: "Why is it architecture?" Or perhaps, more specifically in the case of this book: "Why is it architectural education?"

Editors Harriet Harriss and Lynnette Widder position Live Projects at the juncture of academia and the profession, making a case for a hybrid of the pedagogical and the practical. As such, the appropriate arenas for architectural education are questioned in relationship to the expanded role of architect, an economically precarious profession, and a thoroughly global practice. Here, we need to rethink this increased complexity and understand it not as a formal pursuit but rather as a density of relationships and connections that increase not only discourse but dialogue.

Hybridity is hardly a neutral stance. For instance, Charles Jencks, in his new introduction to *Adhocism*, reissued by MIT Press, describes the book's title as a "mongrel term" and of the subject writes, "it prospers like most hybrids on the edge of respectability" (Jencks and Silver 2013: vii). With the power of "both/and" – that is, Live Projects embrace the best of design speculation, sociological strategies, and construction technique – comes the specter of "neither/nor" – that these projects are compromised by their lack of trajectory within an avant-gardist pursuit.

Later, in the second half of *Adhocism* (part of the original 1971 edition), co-author Nathan Silver uncovers why hybridity jangles nerves and finds its potential for systemic transformation in his "An appreciation of hybrid forms." He writes: "[p]ractical adhocism inevitably has to do with impure, bastard systems, because one order linked to another order disturbs the serene autonomy of reach . . .. What first seemed grotesque eventually becomes normal. Thus successive barriers of formal inhibitions collapse" (Jencks and Silver 2013: 140).

So, ultimately, hybridity not only identifies the parts within established systems that leave not only openings (wittingly or unwittingly) for appropriation – an instructor's willingness to explore design briefs that expand outside the studio setting or an applied use of computational tools in service to larger community – but also the exciting possibility that "the rub" of Live Projects becomes unexceptional, even normative.

References

Jencks, C., and Silver, N. (2013). *Adhocism: The Case for Improvisation*, MIT Press.
Kennedy, R. (2013). "Outside the Citadel, Social Practice Art is Intended to Nurture," *New York Times*, March 20, 2013. Available online at: http://www.nytimes.com/2013/03/24/arts/design/outside-the-citadel-social-practice-art-is-intended-to-nurture.html?pagewanted=all Accessed January 2013.

ACKNOWLEDGEMENTS

The editors wish to acknowledge the support of Head of School Matt Gaskin at Oxford Brookes School of Architecture, UK, and the Masters of Sustainability Management programme at Columbia University, USA.

INTRODUCTION

Pedagogy into practice ... or practice into pedagogy?

Harriet Harriss and Lynnette Widder

The book's bold aim is simple: to provide a persuasive, evidence-based advocacy for moving a particular kind of architectural learning known as Live Projects away from the realm of provocation and marginality into a position of belonging – towards a holistic integration into current and future architectural curricula. Live Projects occupy the borderlands between the simulacra which architectural education favors – the speculative project, supported by lecture and seminar-based exercises – and the trial by fire of professional practice. Because of this position, Live Projects as a vehicle for providing teaching and service simultaneously has the potential to recalibrate the contesting claims that both academia and profession make on architecture. Many of the chapters in this book argue persuasively that Live Projects create channels for a new, reciprocal influence from pedagogy to practice – or is it practice to pedagogy?

As editors and authors, we have collected essays and case studies that consider how Live Projects address issues often glossed over in traditional architectural education and speculate on the pressures exerted by the integration of Live Projects into existing architectural curricula and teaching methods. We also reflect upon how the rising demand for an architecture education that involves distributed authorship, self-advocacy, and other collaboration-based values can be addressed through Live Projects and the lessons they teach. Neither fully academic nor proto-professional, Live Projects have the capacity to carry the virtues of both spheres while sensitizing students to the shortcomings inherent to the arbitrary, albeit necessary, separation between the two. As a teaching method and introduction to professional practice, Live Projects are already well established in other professional education tracks, including business, law, journalism, public health, and management. This book is evidence of how they can productively assert themselves in architecture as well.

How we conceive the book

Drawing upon its beginnings in the Oxford Brookes University 2012 Live Projects conference call for papers, chaired by Harriet Harriss, this book refines thematic and practical alignment, to contextualize each author's assertions. The results are of real value to current and aspirational Live Projects practitioners as models, references, and larger pedagogic considerations. Each contribution considers different facets of theory, logistics, and physical outcomes which, taken together, will allow Live Projects to gain wider and more effective usage. Some chapters describe structural models for academic administrators; others explore appropriate learning theory references; still others depict case study projects, models for accreditation, speculations on beauty and utility, proposals for the common good. Together, they define a network of concerns and knowledge around Live Projects.

An overview of content

The book is made up of longer essays, grouped thematically, and a series of reference case studies towards its end. Part I, entitled "Theories, models, and manifestos," includes information that we believe is foundational to Live Projects practice. Jane Anderson and Colin Priest discuss the OB1 LIVE Project, a series of Live Projects which they treated as a control set over the course of years, testing and evaluating different constellations within a consistent student cohort. They discuss their findings using the metric of situated learning theory, an established body of pedagogic knowledge suited to Live Projects but otherwise only casually considered relative to the teaching of architecture. James Benedict Brown's chapter identifies a larger spectrum of learning theories relevant to Live Projects, then directly cross-references them to his substantial research on UK architectural education. Megan Clark, the manager of strategic partnerships for the Engage office at the California College of the Arts, uses her account of a specific partnered project for a not-for-profit to describe in depth the very successful project development scaffold that CCA uses and the social value it generates. Lynnette Widder, also a US academic at a private university, describes the imperative to participate in Live Projects and the way the integration of Live Projects can challenge and ultimately advance the practice of architectural education. This part of the book concludes with Harriet Harriss' reflective analysis of how a manifesto proves a highly effective agent in advancing an erudite entreaty for an incipient Live Project assessment strategy.

"The question of assessment," Part II of the book, interrogates the RIBA accreditation requirements and their US equivalent, the NAAB rubric. David Gloster, the Director of Education for RIBA, confronts directly the contention that Live Projects are located outside, or in conflict with, the primary intentions behind accreditation. He also makes a case for another central concern of architectural education that likewise cannot be explicitly quantified by accreditation criteria – beauty. Christine Theodoropoulos, the Dean of the School of

Architecture at Cal Poly San Luis Obispo and a practiced leader of NAAB accreditation teams, argues that Live Projects have been embraced and mainstreamed by American accreditation and intern development programs which recognize the diverse contributions that Live Projects make to the education of architects. Alan Chandler, from the University of East London, takes a different tack, claiming that only explicit mention in formal terms of accreditation can insure the uptake of Live Projects by compelling schools to properly fund and staff these highly labor- and material-intensive undertakings. Niles Gore's research gives historical context to the questions Live Projects pose to assumptions about how and how much construction knowledge an architect should have: Gore locates the roots of this debate in the US within the immediate post-war period.

The chapters in Part III, "From Education into Practice," capture Live Projects that are deliberately located either physically or philosophically between the academy and the world of practice. Alex MacLaren discusses Teambuild, a UK interdisciplinary annual competition for young professionals that addresses the need for the collaboration and flexible decision-making required of built environment professionals. TeamBuild models multifactorial and fast-paced challenges in a collegial teaching environment. Sebastian Messer describes the innovative GRAD program, born of necessity to offer recent graduates a professional support system for completing community-based self-projects but now evolved into a vital practice/academy partnership that resolves such thorny issues as liability, knowledge transfer, and best practices. Beverly Sandalack's chapter on UrbanLab offers an approach to paraprofessional Live Projects that can speed the uptake of academic research. Working in Canada at an urban scale, UrbanLab offers faculty and professionally supported environments for recent grads to complete projects with community and social agendas, in some cases leading to paid and realized work. Although socially responsible design and community engagement are not the *sine qua non* of Live Projects, these examples model the positive potentials for proto-professional service to provide for a better built environment among non-traditional clients. In a more overtly polemic vein, Barnaby Bennett and Ryan Reynolds see Live Projects as a springboard to what they call "radical practice." Christian Volkmann, reflecting on the role that Live Projects play in conveying to students the challenges of moving from planning to realization, cites his own experiences and follow-up research with the US Solar Decathlon in 2011–12.

Part IV communicates the virtues of Live Projects through a series of case studies. It presents a series of projects that populate the field of Live Projects in an organized, surveyable manner. Current and aspiring Live Projects practitioners, whether students, faculty, academic administrators, young professionals, or architectural practices, will find precedents relevant to their interests and concerns. Without claiming to be comprehensive, this collection represents a start at describing by example what can be included within the compass of "Live Projects." It also offers powerful evidence that neither social responsibility nor good design need be sacrificed.

Michael Hughes discusses the work currently being done at full scale in his home institution, the American University of Sharjah. Bruce Wrightsman, now of Kansas State University, describes a collaboration between the University of Montana (his previous university) and the US National Forests Service to develop a new structure within a spectacular, relatively inaccessible landscape; the students involved were able to provide a new interpretation of the strict Forest Service architectural guidelines and in turn gained the opportunity to learn stone cutting, masonry, and craft-quality carpentry. Ann Markey, from a UK point of view, describes a series of architecturally significant projects that have successfully dovetailed Live Projects and the demands of post-graduation professional licensure. In contrast to one-off approaches to Design-Build Live Projects, the New York Institute of Technology has already realized a series of complete buildings with a sustainability focus, as Frank Mruk, the Associate Dean of Architecture at that school, explains. Sophie Davies' chapter is written from the perspective of a student participant in disaster relief-based Live Projects staged out-of-area in India. Students' ability to reverse the design process by beginning with the purchase of inexpensive materials for an interior fit-out in the Fareshare Project is the basis for Simon Warren's assertions about the pedagogic value of Live Projects, which he reinforces with quotations from recent literature. Natasha Lofthouse and Charlie Fisher offer another student perspective, reflecting upon how they worked far beyond their academic and assessment calendar to deliver meaningful outcomes for a school client in Oxford, UK. Professor Christopher Livingston and student Shauntel Nelson reflect upon an historic Live Project at their US land-grant university. The case studies conclude with Prue Chiles' chapter on the importance of civic engagement at close range within a global society based upon multifarious Live Project outputs at Sheffield University.

The final section of the book contains two reflective pieces on Live Projects. The first captures a conversation between two practitioners whose teaching and professional work is intertwined with various kinds of Live Project: Alfred Zollinger of Matter Practice in Brooklyn, New York, and Daisy Froud of Agents of Change in London consider the way questions of agency, the one-to-one, risk-taking, and discovery can play out in a series of Live Projects contexts. The book concludes with Mel Dodd's thoughts on the importance of generating alternative and diverse models of pedagogy as a means to enable and sustain more diverse forms of practice.

How we hope it will be used

The sections into which the chapters have been placed sketch the topics and challenges we foresee and should assist the reader in locating what is useful. The book can be read cover-to-cover as a narrative woven from theory to implementation, from the academy to practice, through the interstices in which Live Projects put down roots. It may serve as a methods tool for educators, and inform assessment and learning outcome design. It is a snapshot of the current status of Live Projects, primarily but not exclusively in the UK and North America. It is also intended to act as a lobbyist manifesto for change, solidifying the gains made and advocating for the ongoing uptake and recognition of this form of teaching in architecture. Finally, it also reflects on the relationship between Live Projects and professional practice, as perceived from both academic and professional perspectives.

Practice and pedagogy

The elephant in the room is, of course, whether Live Projects ultimately make for "better" graduates, on the one hand, and a "better" architectural practice environment, on the other. Certainly Live Projects can provide vital client education upon which later consultancies can build. At this moment, however, there is a dearth of metrics, let alone research, to track the reciprocity between practice and pedagogy via Live Projects. From what benchmark should change be measured? What constitutes better? And who says that things as they stand need improvement?

One area in which the power of Live Projects can be most easily assessed is an area with which our profession seems to struggle more than most: the problem of heroic authorship and deep personal identification with one's own work. In the appropriate measure, empathy with a project is highly motivating and gratifying; heroizing originality and ingenuity puts emphasis on the strengths of a creative professional track. On the other hand, fixation on authorship and mark-making does not motivate collaboration, open-mindedness, or good communication. As the authors in this book all argue, these three activities are at the crux of the successful Live Project. This fact is bolstered by Live Projects teaching in other professions, which often require strictly hierarchical structures of students to define each person's role in the team.

As Live Projects assert themselves – in part through the efforts of the authors assembled here and of books such as this – we look forward to seeing how this gauntlet is taken up by practice and by pedagogy.

PART I

Theories, models, and manifestos

1.1

DEVELOPING AN INCLUSIVE DEFINITION, TYPOLOGICAL ANALYSIS AND ONLINE RESOURCE FOR LIVE PROJECTS

Jane Anderson and Colin Priest

Introduction

What makes a project live? How do you structure a Live Project? How do Live Projects relate to education, practice and the community?

This chapter describes the experimentation with and documentation and analysis of a diverse range of Live Projects, discussed in relation to Lave and Wenger's theory of situated learning via a process of legitimate peripheral participation (Lave and Wenger 1996) and findings from OB1 LIVE (Anderson and Priest 2013a), the authors' programme of Live Projects. From this work we devised an inclusive definition and method of typological analysis that revealed different Live Project models and previously concealed connections between them. This was tested, expanded and disseminated through our development of the Live Projects Network (Anderson and Priest 2013b), an online resource to recognise and connect the multiplicity of participants in Live Project practice.

Initial empirical findings: OB1 LIVE and six factors common to all Live Projects

Our initial analysis of Live Project types and pedagogies came from observations made as tutors running Live Projects with our students (Anderson and Priest 2012). The projects described below demonstrate the reasoning behind our identification of six factors needed to make a project 'live'.

In 2008 we established OB1 LIVE, a programme of Live Projects commissioned by community-based clients and designed by year one students of architecture and interior architecture at Oxford Brookes School of Architecture. Our first observations of students' response to participation in Live Projects echoed the findings of Morrow, Parnell and Torrington (Morrow *et al.* 2004: 98), who describe the high levels of confidence and motivation of their year one architecture students at the University of Sheffield when participating in projects devised to connect creativity and reality.

The existence of a real brief and a tangible end product was clearly important in making our Live Projects meaningful for our students. The first OB1 LIVE Project was 'Sounds of the Place' for the 2008 National Architecture Student Festival, London. This followed a familiar "live build" format: a group of students volunteer to construct a temporary installation in a public place in response to a brief set by a student architecture festival. Our familiar role as studio tutors had shifted to that of agents (Anderson and Priest 2012: 54), guiding students through the uncertainties of the building process, including its financial and temporal realities. We realised that it was important to value uncertainty and leave space for a dynamic and non-linear pedagogic model specific to Live Projects.

We wished to establish a workable structure for curricular projects that involved the entire cohort and not just a self-selecting group of enthusiastic volunteers. There was little literature available on the pedagogy of architectural Live Projects and no agreed definition of what a Live Project actually was. Our understanding was similar to that described by Sara: 'The Live Project is . . . a type of design project that is distinct from a typical studio project in its engagement of real clients or users, in real-time settings' (Sara 2006: 1). Our second 2008 project, 'Weather Stations', required us to question what was achievable with year one students. The brief was for environmental educational play structures for a new garden at the Donnington Doorstep Family Centre. Very clear parameters were set for this project. We pre-negotiated access to the clients and site, drew up a brief, including a budget, with an agreed product and set a defined start and end point for the project. This project set a template for those to follow and retrospectively we can identify six factors that we consider are common to all Live Projects: external collaborator, educational organisation, brief, timescale, budget and product.

Development

Pedagogical context: situated learning via peripheral participation

In their book *Situated Learning: Legitimate Peripheral Participation*, analysing five case studies of different apprenticeship models internationally, Lave and Wenger point out that all learning is situated, regardless of its context. They observed that 'learners inevitably participate in communities of practitioners and that mastery of knowledge and skill requires newcomers to move toward full participation in the sociocultural practices of a community' (Lave and Wenger 1996: 29). We noted that 'during a Live Project a mutual trust is built up between students and tutors that motivates learning and starts to develop a shared exploration of what the design process involves and what it is to practice as an architect' (Anderson and Priest 2012: 53). Lave and Wenger's statement 'As opportunities for understanding how well or poorly one's efforts contribute are evident in practice, legitimate participation of a peripheral kind provides an immediate ground for self-evaluation' (Lave and

Wenger 1996: 111) is a potent description of a positive learning cycle where feedback is obtained *in situ* and is made significant by its authentic context, and where learning is absorbed by the learner willingly and informs their future practice and own critical judgement.

Live Projects are perceived by some as being too technically or sociologically complex for year one or even undergraduate students to tackle (Jeremy Till pers. comm. at the 2012 *Architecture 'Live Projects' Pedagogy* International Symposium). However, Lave and Wenger point out the important role that learners can play within society and their chosen profession. 'Legitimate peripherality is important for developing "constructively naïve" perspectives or questions. From this point of view, inexperience is an asset to be exploited. It is of use, however, only in the context of participation, when supported by experienced practitioners who both understand its limitations and value its role' (Lave and Wenger 1996: 117). With a low-to-no budget and inexperienced cohort, OB1 LIVE Projects looked very different from the typical 'live build' projects seen in the architectural press (Stacey 2009: 14–15). We were forced to question what defined a project as 'live'.

Definition

Documentation, reflection and analysis: OB1 LIVE blog

The next phase of research comprised documentation on our OB1 LIVE blog (Anderson and Priest 2013a) (see Figure 1.1.1) and reflection on twelve OB1 LIVE Projects carried out between 2008 and 2011 (Anderson and Priest 2012). This was combined with experimentation with, and analysis of, different project formats, using them to test different hypotheses. Some of the six factors that we eventually recognised as being common to all Live Projects (brief, product, external collaborator, timescale, budget, educational organisation) were more difficult to identify than others.

Brief: By running a combination of live and traditional design studio projects we observed that both types could include a real brief and site. Without further factors it would be impossible to distinguish them (Mount Place, 2009).

Product: There is a common expectation that the outcome of a live architectural project must be a building but this is not even the case in many professional projects, where the outcome can be feasibility studies, ideas generation (Film Oxford, 2010) or prototypes (Donnington Doorstep, 2008). We realised that Live Projects could end at any point in a similar way to professional projects but that the outcome must be recognised and presented as a product.

External collaborator: An important question was 'Does there need to be a client to make a project live?' We tested this in 2011 with 'Now Showing', a self-initiated on-campus pop-up cinema project. Although at first this project did not appear to have a client, we observed that students were still designing for a user – their fellow students on campus. They were also required to satisfy the demands of the university campus managers – effectively a client with its own needs to meet. On

OB1 LIVE

Menu
About
News
Contact
Contributors
Participants
Links

Welcome to the website and archive for OB1 LIVE projects.

OB1 LIVE is an innovative programme of design projects commissioned by community based clients and created by students of architecture at Oxford Brookes University. OB1 LIVE was founded by architects Jane Anderson and Colin Priest.

Index

FIGURE 1.1.1   Screenshot of the OB1 LIVE website taken on 26 June 2013.

balance, even this self-initiated project revealed de facto external collaborators for the students to work with.

Timescale: This is an inevitable factor and it can be difficult to make Live Projects fit within the academic calendar. We found that a broader view of the possibilities inherent to the other factors, particularly brief, product and external collaborator, enabled more imaginative ways to achieve this (The Story Museum, 2011–12).

Budget: A budget is also inevitable but often overlooked, particularly when operating on a make do and mend or exchange basis, as many Live Projects do (Found! 2013).

Educational organisation: Another question that arose in a 2009 project, 'Tactile model for the blind', was 'Are student-led projects live?' This was a very small-scale extra-curricular commission undertaken by two students. Our very limited involvement to negotiate the terms of the project meant that this was a very marginal case, moving closer to practice than education. The involvement of an educational organisation is a critical factor in distinguishing a Live Project from a professional one.

We had identified six factors common to all Live Projects and tested them to ensure that they offered flexibility in their application to different situations. Through a consideration of their inter-relationship in the context of learning, we formed an inclusive definition of a Live Project: 'A Live Project comprises the negotiation of a brief, timescale, budget and product between an educational organisation and an external collaborator for their mutual benefit. The project must be structured to ensure that students gain learning that is relevant to their educational development.'

Dissemination

Typological analysis and online resource: Live Projects Network

In 2012 we established the Live Projects Network (Anderson and Priest 2013b), an international online network of Live Projects to connect students, academics, practitioners and external collaborators involved in Live Projects (see Figure 1.1.). The purpose is to promote the use of Live Projects in education, share best practice, encourage dialogue and contribute to the establishment of a theoretical basis for the study of Live Projects. The site aims to include as diverse a series of case studies as possible for different Live Project models.

From an initial analysis of the first fifteen different Live Project case studies on the network from Oxford Brookes University, McGill School of Architecture, Montreal, and the University of Portsmouth we saw that even very diverse project types shared the six factors that we had identified. Each factor comprised its own spectrum of variables. For example, the nature of the relationship with the external collaborator could range from a commission to a collaboration to a self-initiated project (see Figure 1.1.3). What differentiated each project was where it sat on each of the six spectra.

By January 2014 twenty-eight educational organisations had contributed seventy-two Live Projects located in seventeen countries in Asia, Europe, America, Africa, and Australia to the Live Projects Network site. These points were used to create a pro forma for contributors to the online Live Projects Network and also as filters so that visitors to the site could find projects with resources similar to their own. This allowed projects that might initially appear to be very different in nature to be connected and understood by others planning their own Live Projects (see Figure 1.1.4).

By July 2013, eighteen educational organisations had contributed fifty-one Live Projects located in twelve countries to the Live Projects Network site. We adapted the terminology of two of the six original factors in response to the variation in Live Project types that we found. This also made our method of analysis more applicable to other disciplines. 'Institution' has become 'educational organisation', to enable us to acknowledge an expanded range of levels of student involved in Live Projects such as Studio H, a public high school 'design/build' programme at http://realmcharterschool.org (accessed January 2014) in Berkeley, California (Millar and Pilloton 2013). It also enabled us to include extra-curricular Live

FIGURE 1.1.2 Screenshot of the Live Projects Network website on 23 July 2013.

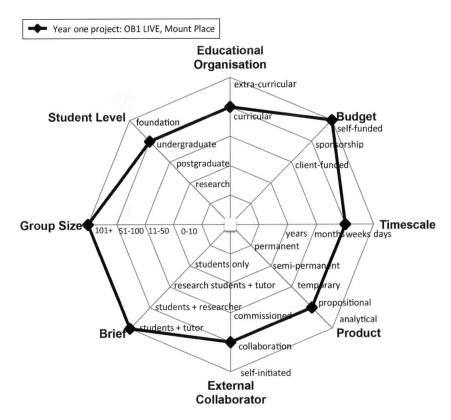

FIGURE 1.1.3 A typical year one project plotted against each of the six spectra common to all Live Projects.

Projects organised by groups connected with educational institutions but with some degree of independence from them, such as volunteer programmes, educational trusts or charities. Similarly, 'client' has become 'external collaborator' to acknowledge non-architectural Live Projects and reflect the collaborative ways of working, modes of mutual exchange and self-initiated projects that are the basis of so many Live Projects, rather than a more conventional client relationship and model for the commissioning of projects.

We can now begin to identify commonly occurring Live Project models that have developed in response to particular conditions. Figure 1.1.4 shows the profile of three different project types: a temporary year one project; a permanent postgraduate project; and a postgraduate applied research project.

As the points along each of the spectra move closer to the centre, projects get closer to a profile that is more typical of a professional project in relation to budget, external collaborator, brief and level. Therefore the year one project is more likely to occupy the outer edge and the postgraduate projects to be closer to the centre. Conversely, some of the more radical contemporary models of practice would break

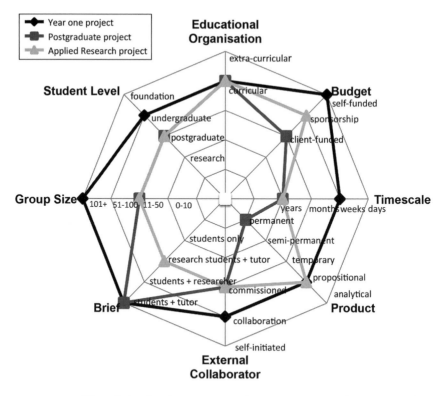

FIGURE 1.1.4 The relationship between typical year one, postgraduate and applied research Live Project models when plotted against each of the six spectra common to all Live Projects.

this mould and move outwards from the centre. However, all projects – studio, live and professional – will occupy the full spectrum in terms of timescale, product, and group size. A year one project can move closer to the centre of the diagram, particularly for small-scale projects.

Conclusion

From our peripheral position, from observation of the practice of others and our own, and from the development of an inclusive definition and typological analysis for universal application to Live Projects we observed the potential of Live Projects for more meaningful learning. The multiplicity of Live Project models suggested that there was a new community of Live Project practitioners who could find mutual benefit by becoming connected. We hypothesise that Live Projects create ideal conditions for situated learning through legitimate peripheral participation and for new relationships between tutor, student and community. Lave and Wenger describe that the 'ambiguous potentitialities of legitimate peripherality reflect the concept's pivotal role in providing access to a nexus of relations otherwise not perceived as connected' (Lave and Wenger 1996: 36). We wish to encourage interdisciplinary and professional discourse across institutions (Anderson 2013), enrich student learning and make Live Projects more accessible to students, tutors, researchers and external collaborators.

We developed the Live Projects Network as an online resource of case studies to connect participants and demonstrate the diversity of Live Project practice. It is a source of information for newcomers that demonstrates ways to work within similar contexts and resources. It connects individuals, disciplines, and institutions, enabling new collaborations and stimulating discourse and best practice.

References

Anderson, J. and Priest, C. (2012). 'The live education of an architect: John Hejduk and OB1 LIVE, imagination and action'. *Journal for Education in the Built Environment*, 7(2). Available online at: http://cebe.cf.ac.uk/jebe/pdf/JaneAnderson7(2).pdf Accessed January 2014.

Anderson, J. (2013). 'Undercurrent: swimming away from the design studio'. In AAE (Association of Architectural Educators), AAE Conference 2013. Nottingham Trent University, 3–5 April 2013.

Anderson, J. and Priest, C. (2013a). *OB1 LIVE*. Available online at: http://www.architecture.brookes.ac.uk/galleries/ob1/index.html Accessed January 2014.

Anderson, J. and Priest, C. (2013b). *Live Projects Network*. Available online at: http://liveprojectsnetwork.org Accessed January 2014.

Lave, J. and Wenger, E. (1996). *Situated Learning. Legitimate Peripheral Participation*. Cambridge: Cambridge University Press.

Millar, M. and Pilloton, E. (2013). Project H Design, A 501c3 nonprofit organization. Available online at: http://www. projecthdesign.org/#studio-h Accessed January 2014.

Morrow, R., Parnell, R. and Torrington, J. (2004). 'Reality versus creativity?' *CEBE Transactions*, 1(2): December. Available online at: http://www.cebe.heacademy. ac.uk/transactions/pdf/RuthMorrow.pdf Accessed January 2014.

Sara, R. (2006). *Live Project Good Practice: A Guide for the Implementation of Live Projects*. CEBE Briefing Guide No. 8. Available online at: http://www.heacademy.ac.uk/assets/documents/subjects/cebe/BriefingGuide_08.pdf Accessed January 2014.

Stacey, M. (2009) 'Nottingham students put this South African community on a learning curve'. *Building Design*, 19 June 2009, pp. 14–15. Available online at: http://www.bdonline.co.uk/buildings/technical/nottingham-students-put-this-south-african-community-on-a-learning-curve/3142913.article Accessed January 2014.

1.2

LEARNING THEORIES FOR LIVE PROJECTS

James Benedict Brown

Introduction

Live Projects are widespread in architectural education, yet they have not been extensively theorized (Albrecht 1988; Erdman and Weddle 2002; Watt and Cottrell 2006; Morrow 2007; Morrow and Brown 2012). This chapter explores two tensions affecting the development of sustainable Live Project pedagogies: firstly, a tension between process and product that must be acknowledged when distinguishing design/build projects from a larger category of Live Projects; and, secondly, a tension between two theoretical categories: complicated pedagogies and complex pedagogies. Through an exploration of these distinctions, architectural educators are encouraged to actively critique their own teaching practice in the development of pedagogies appropriate for Live Projects in architectural education.

The opinions of architectural educators

This chapter emerges from a period of research that developed a grounded theory of Live Projects that invited architectural educators to describe and critique their understanding and experiences of Live Projects. (Brown 2012) Following a postal survey of every validated or recognized architecture course in the UK and Republic of Ireland, a sample of twenty-one architectural educators at seventeen Higher Education institutions was collated. All respondents, interviewed individually between September and November 2010 using a semi-structured interview schedule, had some current or previous experience in the delivery of Live Projects in architectural education. Building on a conception of grounded theory methodology set out by Charmaz (2005; 2006) and in order to make manageable the sheer volume of the data collected, a four-stage coding process was deployed. Beginning with a line-by-line analysis of the transcribed interviews, individual codes (active statements describing actions, processes or emotions of a single line of transcribed interview) were generated. Related or similar codes were grouped together to form concepts. Broader groups of concepts were then clustered around categories which were finally explained by emergent theories. Twenty-four discrete theories were thus generated from more than 150,000 words of transcribed interviews (Brown 2012).

In examining the role of the Live Project in British and Irish architectural education, a tension immediately emerges between process and product. When asked to name notable Live Project precedents, respondents most frequently cited the Rural Studio of Auburn University, Alabama, an American design-build studio (Rural Studio 2013). Yet fewer than 10 per cent of the same sample considered construction to be an essential component of the Live Project. In light of this observation, it is important to differentiate design-build projects from the larger category of Live Projects, as in both the literature (Sara 2006; Watt and Cottrell 2006; Morrow and Brown 2012) and this research the architecture Live Project is primarily defined in terms of students experiencing not actual construction but a working relationship with an external client. This is especially important given that 'the natural default of most architects and architectural educators is to give preference to the delivery of a product' (Morrow 2007: 278).

The limitations of complicated pedagogies

How may architectural educators go about theorizing the Live Project, especially given that the participation of a third party (the client) renders many binary (teacher–student) pedagogical theories inappropriate? This chapter builds upon a distinction set forward by Davis *et al.* (2000) between two pedagogical categories: complicated and complex. Complicated pedagogies seek 'to reduce phenomena to elemental components, root causes, and fundamental laws' (ibid.: 62), whereas complex pedagogies 'suggest that learning is not about acquiring or accumulating information. Rather, learning is principally a matter of keeping pace with one's evolving circumstances' (ibid.: 78). This chapter argues that architectural educators who wish to develop their own pedagogical approaches to Live Projects should distinguish these two categories and the limitations of their respective theories.

Two notable complicated pedagogies appropriate to architectural education are Schön's theory of reflective learning and Kolb's Experiential Learning Model. In *The Reflective Practitioner* Schön (1983) proposes that one-to-one design studio tuition is effective precisely because it simulates professional architectural practice. Till (2005) notes that Schön's theorizing of the one-to-one design tutorial was received uncritically by the architectural profession 'because it supports the status quo, and since that support comes from a distinguished outsider it gives it a special credence' (ibid.: 167). Schön describes a one-to-one design studio tutorial between a male architecture professor (Quist) and a female student (Petra). Quist's internalized reframing and re-designing of both the design problem and the design itself 'takes the form of a reflective conversation with the situation' (ibid.: 241–2). By taking control of the design problem, Quist is seen to reframe it based on his experience and knowledge and to work through the consequences of potential alternatives in 'a situation of complexity and uncertainty which demands the imposition of an order' (ibid.: 103). Schön celebrates Quist's 'unfailing virtuosity', suggesting uncritically that it is through the one-to-one tutorial situation that a student of architecture may best assimilate the mastery of problem-solving through design.

Although Dewey (1963) first described an epistemology of experience several decades earlier, the first pedagogical framework to closely theorize the function of experience in learning was David Kolb's Experiential Learning Model (ELM). Kolb (1984) describes experiential learning as a personal and developmental cycle of four stages linking concrete experience, reflective observation, abstract conceptualization, and active experimentation. The learner experiences, interprets, generalizes, and then applies their newly found knowledge. Critics of Kolb's ELM (Holman *et al.* 1997; Miettinen 2000; Beard and Wilson 2006) share similar concerns: that the syncretic development of a pedagogical framework is eclectic, insufficiently critical, and, crucially, 'a minimalist interpretation of the complex operations of the brain' (Holman *et al.* 1997: 43).

In spite of these criticisms, Schön's theory of reflective learning and Kolb's ELM are highly suited to the study of Live Project learning since they propose sequential frameworks that theorize the process by which an individual learns, examining the role of personal experience and personal reflection in a sequence of experience, reflection, and action. But these frameworks fail to attend to a wider context of learning beyond the individual, including the effects of the hidden curriculum, 'those unstated values, attitudes, and norms which stem tacitly from social relations of the school and classroom as well as the content of the course' (Dutton 1991: 167). The reflective learning that Schön describes is little more than a kind of osmosis, in which the student is expected to watch, repeat, and understand how a more experienced tutor handles a design problem. Webster (2008) notes that it pays no attention to the social, cultural, and experience differential between them. Furthermore, it remains dependent on a binary student–teacher relationship and a teaching environment that supports one-to-one tuition, making it increasingly obsolete in higher education today. While Kolb's ELM embeds action and reflection in the cycle of learning, the cycle is conceived purely in terms of individual learning and development, and does not provide practical tools for theorizing either the inter-disciplinary practice of the architect or the collaborative learning of the Live Project.

The opportunities of complexity

By focusing on internalized processes, Schön's theory of reflective learning and Kolb's ELM overlook the great potential of the design studio to be theorized as a holistic learning environment. The very nature of the design studio as a project-based learning space can thwart attempts to make sense of it through complicated pedagogies. The recognition that 'knowledge is contingent, contextual, and evolving; never absolute, universal, or fixed' (Davis *et al.* 2000: 78) leads to the exploration of complex pedagogies that recognize the interrelationship and interdependency between learners and teachers and a constantly evolving and contingent learning environment. In these terms, 'learning is coming to be understood as a participation in the world, a co-evolution of knower and known that transforms both' (ibid.: 64). An example of how architectural education can be reshaped to support such an understanding of learning is the Women's School of Planning and Architecture (WSPA). The WSPA was a summer school held five times between 1975 and 1981 (Records of the Women's School of Planning and Architecture n.d.). It sought 'to create a forum within which we may discover and define the particular qualities, concerns, and abilities that we as women bring to the environmental design professions' (Weisman *et al.*: 10). At the time, fewer than 10 per cent of practising architects and 1 per cent of architectural academics in America were women. Leslie Kanes Weisman explains that the 'WSPA would not duplicate what was available in a traditional academic setting' and that 'form, content, and context have to have a kind of consistency' (ibid.). To that end, the WSPA was conceived as a non-hierarchical learning environment with no distinction between teachers and students. There was no externalized body of knowledge to be acquired. The pedagogical model of the design studio was subtly altered in order to develop a more democratic and coherent relationship between pedagogical process and product. To support this, the WSPA was organized around a communal school schedule to which all participants were allowed to make changes or additions. Core courses deliberately overlapped to encourage the merging of apparently unrelated sessions.

While the WSPA demonstrated how students and teachers might take ownership of a pedagogical space, how might architectural educators develop formal approaches to teaching and learning that are suitable for less radical academic environments? To give just one example of a complex pedagogy informing how we develop our own pedagogies of Live Projects, Ruth Morrow and I have argued elsewhere (Morrow and Brown 2012) that such projects may be theorized as examples of critical pedagogy, especially when compared with the predominant transmission model (or, according to Freire (1996), the 'banking model') of education. In the Live Project, the binary teacher–student relationship is subverted, not only with the introduction of a client who is external to the academic environment but also with the recognition that every Live Project participant may bring unique skills and knowledge to the process. Crysler warns that 'constituting the student as voiceless and the teacher as speech-enabler returns the teacher to the position of dominance that critical pedagogy claims to challenge' (1995: 213), and argues that critical pedagogy must be theorized in relation to the institutional context of the academy, cautioning that 'if students investigate society without questioning the position they occupy in doing so, the role of the distanced expert is reinforced rather than questioned. The "social" and its human contents will continue to appear as objectified problems rather than as representations of problems in which the positions of both observer and observed are constructed' (ibid.). Working with, for, and alongside their client, Live Project students must be supported in a negotiation between two value systems: an academic value system by which their work will be assessed and their clients' non-academic value system by which the brief will be satisfied. The Live Project has been recognized for creating a context for learning that is 'between the studio and the street' (Sara 2004: 245), but architectural educators who employ Live Projects must ask whether they are an excursion of the design studio into the street or an opportunity for 'the street' to enter the design studio. And, more importantly, on whose terms and according to whose values is the interaction mediated (Brown in press)?

Conclusion

Attempts to develop complicated pedagogies of architectural education struggle precisely because they tend to focus their attentions on either the internalized processes of experience and reflection or the binary teacher–student learning relationship, thereby neglecting the complex overlapping contexts of education (Webster 2008). Complex pedagogies such as those developed at the WSPA propose alternatives to normative models of architectural education by subverting the division between pedagogical content and form. Likewise, Live Projects in architectural education blur the distinction between process and product. It would be apposite to suggest that Live Projects are difficult to theorize as examples of complicated pedagogies precisely because they are so highly situated and contingent upon the contexts that give them life. The greatest opportunity presented by the Live Project is not that it is a place to reflect on one's own learning but that it is a place to share that learning and reflection with others. By choosing to introduce Live Projects to the academy, we are obliged to critique them. It falls to the architectural educator who employs Live Projects to engage with their complexity in order to theorize and critique their practice.

References

Albrecht, J. (1988). 'Towards a Theory of Participation in Architecture: An Examination of Humanistic Planning Theories'. *Journal of Architectural Education* 42(1): 24–31.

Beard, C., and Wilson, J.P. (2006). *Experiential Learning: A Best Practice Handbook for Educators and Trainers*, 2nd edn. London: Kogan Page.

Brown, J. B. (2012). 'A Critique of the Live Project', PhD thesis, Queen's University Belfast.

Brown, J. B. (in press). '"An output of value" – Exploring the Role of the Live Project as a Pedagogical Bureau de Change'. *Charrette* 1(1).

Charmaz, K. (2005). 'Grounded Theory in the 21st Century'. In *The Sage Handbook of Qualitative Research*, ed. N. K. Denzin and Y. S. Lincoln, 3rd edn. Thousand Oaks, CA: Sage, pp. 507–535.

Charmaz, K. (2006). *Constructing Grounded Theory*. Thousand Oaks, CA: Sage.

Crysler, C. G. (1995). 'Critical Pedagogy and Architectural Education'. *Journal of Architectural Education* 48(4): 208–217.

Davis, B., Sumara, D., and Luce-Kapler, R. (2000). *Engaging Minds: Learning to Teach in Complex Times*. Mahwah, NJ: Lawrence Erlbaum Associates.

Dewey, J. (1963). *Experience & Education*. New York: Collier Books.

Dutton, T. A. (ed.) (1991). *Voices in Architectural Education: Cultural Politics and Pedagogy*. London: Bergin & Garvey.

Erdman, J., and Weddle, R. (2002). 'Designing/Building/Learning'. *Journal of Architectural Education* 55(3): 174–179.

Freire, P. (1996). *Pedagogy of the Oppressed*, new revised edition. Harmondsworth: Penguin.

Haraway, D. (1991). 'Situated Knowledges: The Science Question in Feminism and the Privilege of Partial Perspective'. In *Simians, Cyborgs and Women*. London: Free Association Books, pp. 183–202.

Holman, D., Pavlica, K., and Thorpe, R. (1997). 'Rethinking Kolb's Theory of Experiential Learning in Management Education'. *Management Learning* 28(2): 135–148.

Kolb, D.A. (1984). *Experiential Learning: Experience as the Source of Learning and Development*. London: Prentice-Hall.

Miettinen, R. (2000). 'The Concept of Experiential Learning and John Dewey's Theory of Reflective Thought and Action'. *International Journal of Lifelong Education* 19(1): 54–72.

Morrow, R. (2007). 'Creative Transformations'. In *Design Studio Pedagogy: Horizons for the Future*, ed. A. Salama and N. Wilkinson. Gateshead: Urban International Press, pp. 100–114.

Morrow, R., and Brown, J. B. (2012). 'Live Projects as Critical Pedagogies'. In *Live Projects: Designing with People*, ed. E. Charlesworth, M. Dodd, and F. Harrison, Melbourne: RMIT, pp. 232–247.

Records of the Women's School of Planning and Architecture (n.d.). Sophia Smith Collection, Smith College, Northampton, MA.

Rural Studio (2013). Rural Studio homepage. Available online at: http://www.ruralstudio. org/ Accessed January 2014.

Sara, R. (2004). 'Between Studio and Street: The Role of the Live Project in Architectural Education', PhD thesis, University of Sheffield.

Sara, R. (2006). *CEBE Briefing Guide Series, No. 8: Live Project Good Practice: A Guide for the Implementation of Live Projects*. Plymouth: University of Plymouth.

Schön, D. (1983). *The Reflective Practitioner: How Professionals Think in Action*. London: Temple Smith.

Till, J. (2005). 'Lost Judgement'. In *EAAE Prize 2003–2005 Writings in Architectural Education*, ed. E. Harder. Copenhagen: EAAE, pp. 164–183.

Till, J. (2009). *Architecture Depends*. Cambridge, MA: MIT Press.

Watt, K., and Cottrell, D. (2006). 'Grounding the Curriculum: Learning from Live Projects in Architectural Education'. *International Journal of Learning* 13: 97–104.

Webster, H. (2008). 'Architectural Education after Schön: Cracks, Blurs, Boundaries and Beyond'. *Journal for Education in the Built Environment* 3(2): 63–74.

Weisman, L. K., Cerulli, C., and Kossak, F. (2009). 'Educator, Activist, Politician'. *Field* 3(1): 7–22.

1.3

ENGAGE AT CALIFORNIA COLLEGE OF THE ARTS

A partnership model for addressing community needs with curricular integrity

Megan Clark

Introduction

Housed within the Center for Art and Public Life at California College of the Arts, ENGAGE at CCA connects faculty, students, and outside experts with community partners through semester-long projects that focus on specific needs that are collaboratively identified and defined. It offers an administrative and pedagogical infrastructure within which to cultivate course-based community partnerships that allow organizations to tap into the creative and critical acumen of students and faculty for the mutual benefit of all involved. By prioritizing shared values and strategically guiding pre-project conversations we cultivate custom-fit partnerships whose scope, timeline, and explicit outcomes meet our partners' needs while emphasizing the role of CCA students as creative agents and critical thinkers. This administrative and pedagogical infrastructure allows ENGAGE faculty, students, and community partners to dive headfirst into the complexities of their shared work.

A short story about how it all begins

I was running late, walking hurriedly with my colleague through San Francisco's Mission District in the pouring rain. Tucked along an otherwise dark and residential street was the gate we were searching for, cage-like blue doors crowned by yellow spotlights that barely lit the sidewalk. In the near-darkness, small groups of men waited patiently, bags in hand. There was no buzzer, but someone soon emerged to open the gate. The haphazard gathering glimpsed through the gate revealed itself to be a snaking line: men with cafeteria trays eagerly awaiting a seat in the crowded common room. Their bags were temporarily stowed beneath a bench that ran the length of the concrete courtyard. There was no place left to sit or to call one's own. That night at the Maria and Martha Shelter sparked an invaluable partnership

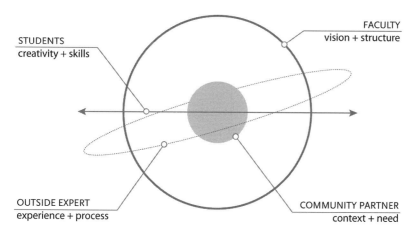

FIGURE 1.3.1   Constellation of ENGAGE at CCA course partners.

with the Dolores Shelter Program (DSP). Along with the Center Director, Sanjit Sethi, and the Interior Design professor Amy Campos, we toured the facility and talked with the DSP's Director, Marlon Mendieta, about how the staff navigates shared and exceedingly public spaces with the adjacent church, daycare, and local union office. When we left, it was with a mutual commitment to reflect on the needs and possibilities that arose; over the next several weeks Professor Campos and I exchanged emails, phone calls, and follow-up visits with Director Mendieta. We determined that students in the first-year Interior Design studio would use their budding design skills to address two basic concerns for the Maria and Martha Shelter: How can the DSP serve more people? And how can they do so while providing an increasing sense of dignity and privacy? The reflections that follow address the challenges and reality of ENGAGE course development that continue to inform the program's ever-evolving model.

Institutional ecology: the Center for Art and Public Life

On the California College of the Arts (CCA) website you will find a quote from the President, Stephen Beal: "CCA's history is tied to the Arts and Crafts movement, a time when artists and designers were producing work that would address the social issues of the time and have a positive impact on the world. This spirit is still very much a part of the college today" (California College of the Arts 2008). Here, President Beal conveys an aspiration to civic ethos that is shared by many institutions of higher education: a belief that academic training necessitates a connection to communities outside the classroom.

In an effort to activate these values, CCA established the Center for Art and Public Life in 1998 as a hub for community-based arts projects. The Center's work was highly successful, ranging from intensive cultural exploration by visiting artists and scholars to neighborhood-specific art workshops. "But," says the Center's Director

Sanjit Sethi, "[they were] less effective at reaching out to the CCA community" (California College of the Arts 2012). Upon taking the helm in 2009, Sethi initiated a shift toward engaging students and faculty as the college's primary agents for addressing concerns raised by San Francisco Bay Area communities. Today, the Center is home to three main programs: ENGAGE at CCA, our focus here; CCA CONNECTS, an externship program; and IMPACT, a social entrepreneurship awards program. Each presents a unique, progressively independent way in which CCA students can apply their creativity and critical insight toward the daily practice and long-term growth of socially invested organizations.

Curricular support

ENGAGE at CCA's core philosophy revolves around the concepts of project-based learning and community engagement. At this intersection, knowledge- and skill-building are significantly enhanced by virtue of being embedded within real-life projects that require students to be accountable to individuals and communities outside the college. The primary challenge, then, comes in developing a dynamic curriculum around a single project for the entire semester, one of the key criteria for an ENGAGE course. The deeper challenge is how to do so while meeting the curricular goals of an academic program. Professor Campos, for example, was required to provide the same technical and theoretical foundation as would any other Interior Design studio course while upholding the commitment to the Dolores Shelter Program.

As a voluntary initiative eager to support project-based community engagement across all 32 academic programs at CCA, ENGAGE sought and received funding to support four faculty mentors, one from each academic division: Architecture, Design, Fine Arts, and Humanities & Sciences. By providing division-specific guidance to fellow faculty on an individual basis, mentors nurture the development of a course or set of courses while simultaneously contributing to a dialogue around the diversity of community engagement practice in creative disciplines. The Center acknowledges that no two ENGAGE courses will have the same depth of relationship or scope of project, and embraces the realities inherent to offering every student at CCA the opportunity to invest themselves in people and places outside the walls of their classroom. It is worth noting that Professor Campos served as mentor for the Architecture Division and that students in Campos' ENGAGE studios have cited these curriculum-enhancing projects as impetus for pursuing further education in community-based practice, including graduate programs in public interest design and public policy (Gonzalez 2011; Patton 2012).

In addition to galvanizing peer mentorship for faculty, ENGAGE seeks out individuals who can augment the expertise of faculty and their partners. The first example of ENGAGE Outside Experts occurred during the initiative's first semester. The faculty member had expertise in landscape design and her community partner had expertise in everything from high school curriculum to youth development, but when it came to designing an intercultural garden they called on an ethno-botanist to work with CCA students and their high school partners. Outside expertise generally falls into one of two categories: content-based, as with the ethno-botanist, or process-based. Noting that content differs from course to course, ENGAGE identifies and funds one to two process-based Outside Experts per semester to help all faculty enhance their community engagement practice. Content-based expertise is sought on an as-needed basis.

Funding

I am frequently asked: How much money can the Center provide for this project? My response is two-fold: the Center is not able to guarantee funding for individual ENGAGE courses, *but* a project will never be green-lighted without ensuring it has the appropriate resources to accomplish its goals. Simply put, we get as much done as we can with what we have, and we begin by assessing the collective resources of our CCA and external partners. Does our community partner have money to contribute to the project? Is the academic program able to contribute for materials or honoraria? This approach acknowledges that the more any partner invests its time, energy, and resources in a project, the more value they are likely to place on the process and outcome surrounding that project.

The Center, meanwhile, asks two additional questions that allow us to take a longer view on project planning and programmatic support. Are there any fundraising opportunities to be undertaken by the Center, or jointly with a particular partner? Is there enough time for faculty to apply for a Curriculum Development Grant through CCA? To date, ENGAGE courses have received funding from private and corporate foundations, including the Adobe Foundation and Panta Rhea, and five faculty have received Curriculum Development Grants from CCA as a direct result of Letters of Support from the Center. These grants have and will cover costs ranging across local travel expenses for youth partners, materials for constructing community development tools, and research around the disparate representation of Arab individuals in the US Census. There are likewise projects, the Dolores Shelter partnership prime among them, where traditional course deliverables such as a full set of design drawings become invaluable fundraising, research, and planning tools in the hands of their community partners. The Center does not pretend that its lean funding model is appropriate for every proposed project, but we maintain that our long-term ability to facilitate meaningful projects at any scale is inextricably linked with our fiscal sustainability.

Cultivating partnerships for the "right fit"

Cultivating partnerships is a year-round, every-day endeavor, tethered to the reality that not every email or phone call leads to a project.

When talking independently with an organization or faculty member about a potential ENGAGE partnership, we emphasize that establishing a course and a project is a relationship-based process that may take several attempts before the right partner emerges. Does the organization actively address social, economic, cultural, or environmental concerns? Is the faculty familiar or comfortable working with non-profit partners? Are the faculty and community partner able to communicate about potential challenges? In spite of our eagerness to realize incredible opportunities, we have to be realistic about the capacity, working style, and vested interest of both parties, and mindful of the time necessary to explore those aspects of the partnership. As in any successful relationship, these discussions uncover organizational priorities and pipe dreams, personal capacity, academic goals, level of urgency, financial considerations, and a host of other details that enable the Center, along with the community partner and faculty member, to determine whether the partnership is the right fit.

Throughout this process we are guided by a series of questions laid out in the ENGAGE at CCA Memorandum of Understanding (MOU). The MOU is a living document that juxtaposes (a) partner introductions, (b) mission statements, (c) course descriptions, and (d) projected deliverables with (e) outlines of partner responsibilities, (f) financial, ownership, and credit considerations, (g) liability notices, and (h) termination criteria. These eight basic sections are completed in tandem with the partnership development process and signed by the faculty member, Center Director, CCA provost, and senior administrator (often the Executive Director) at the community partner organization. This ensures, first and foremost, that we have touched on the practical considerations that have the tendency to get lost in the excitement, as well as confirming that all decision-making parties within the partner organization are aware and supportive of the project. One project drove home the value of this seemingly overly legalized process. A high school administrator reviewing their final MOU draft called to ask who would be paying for the CCA students' fingerprinting and tuberculosis testing, a necessary requirement for all volunteers in the local public school system. It was a key logistical detail of which our primary project liaison, a high school teacher, had been wholly unaware, and one that the MOU process spurred us to resolve promptly.

Shared value/shared risk

Alongside the tangle of face-to-face meetings, site visits, and follow-up emails that establish the practical viability of a project is the parallel quest to find shared value. Will the project provide the community partner with something they otherwise could not have accomplished? Will the students have creative freedom to address their community partner's need? When answered affirmatively – that is, when both sides of the partnership find inherent personal or organizational value in fulfilling their role – these are the questions that uncover the potential for long-lasting impact. The final presentations for the Maria and Martha Shelter were indeed a realization of the potential we had uncovered in our first visit. Mendieta and the DSP's Associate Director were blown away by the students' proposals. The design of space-saving furniture and privacy-providing bunk beds, which enthralled and challenged the first-year students, was something the DSP staff simply didn't have the time to consider.

The necessary co-conspirator to shared value is shared risk. The time and energy spent getting to know one another, trading feedback, and intertwining goals requires faith in the investment of your partner. Students in Professor Campos' class spent the first few weeks of their semester talking with the DSP staff about the shelter system and the social stigma around homelessness, in particular the stigma for men of color and migrant laborers in California, and the safety concerns for transgender individuals who don't fit into the system's tidy gender-segregated protocol. They also learned from shelter residents, whose experiences within that system are bounded by nightly curfews, 7 a.m. checkouts and 90-day maximum stays in buildings that can never truly be called home. They then went to work designing beds that maximized privacy and personal storage while minimizing total floor space, and carefully tessellating bed frames within the shelter's single permanent dormitory to fit in more beds, in some cases making it possible for the DSP to accommodate 20 additional residents in a dignified manner. And what may have seemed like a simple twist to the bed frame design prompted the DSP to ask if they might present the proposals to both the local shelter directors assembly and a national shelter conference as an alternative to the bunk beds currently purchased from the same manufacturers used by the prison system. Mendieta recently stated that the DSP has been able to implement several of the low-cost ideas and that they formally incorporated at least two of the more resource-intensive ideas into their architectural plans (Mendieta 2013). Indeed, the mutual risk of faculty and community partner was validated far beyond the expectations of anyone involved.

Closing

In a recent report, "Community-Partnered Project-Based Studio Pedagogy," Dr. Melanie Corn talks about what she calls "the trope of 'natural ability,'" the belief that the only faculty who can teach these courses have community engagement in their DNA (Corn 2013). However unfounded, it nonetheless leaves interested but uninformed faculty asking themselves: Where do I begin? Could I even do that? Do I need more training? And who should I talk to? The goal of ENGAGE at CCA, as a hub for connecting with community-based organizations and as an evolving educational model, is to help demonstrate "here's how" and "absolutely you can do that."

References

California College of the Arts. (2008). *CCA History*. Available online at: https://www.cca.edu/about/history Accessed January 2014.

California College of the Arts. (2012). *Sanjit Sethi: Community Works*. Available online at: https://www.cca.edu/news/2012/04/23/sanjit-sethi-community-works Accessed January 2014.

Corn, Melanie. (2013). "Community-partnered project-based studio pedagogy: Developing a framework and exploring the impact on faculty in art and design higher education," PhD thesis, University of Pennsylvania.

Gonzalez, Elise. (2011). "Discussion on future plans." Pers. comm., 10 November.

Mendieta, Marlon. (2013). "ENGAGE at CCA: Partnership reflections." Survey response, 9 April.

Patton, Taylor. (2012). "Discussion on future plans." Pers. comm., 1 May.

1.4

WHAT BELONGS TO ARCHITECTURE

Teaching construction among Live Projects

Lynnette Widder

Introduction

The increasing uptake of Live Projects in architectural curricula has repercussions for the way non-studio courses are taught, especially in construction and building technologies. Perhaps more so than any other vehicle for architectural education, Live Projects celebrate the benefits and responsibilities of distributed authorship. Students who have learned first hand the difficulties of precisely completing even rudimentary construction place higher demands on building technologies instruction. They value empirical learning for the inevitable failures it includes; they are able to learn to transpose architectural ideas into their constructed forms, as opposed to the fetishized and copy/paste detailing to which academic construction often defaults.

During my tenure at the Rhode Island School of Design, Live Projects became part of the studio curriculum at all levels and at many different scales, and included the local and out of area, the temporary and permanent. My construction technologies courses were designed to respond to the culture of Live Projects by using their methods in a classroom context.

One course in particular, *Integrated Building Systems* (IBS), exemplifies this response. It was developed with my colleague Andrew Tower, a RISD grad who co-owns a local Providence design/build firm. The course was conceived to train observation, empirical method, and full-scale drawing. It emphasized a temporal dimension in the assembly and life cycle of construction details. We also emphasized systems thinking and drew in guest lectures on microchemistry, environmental ecology, and urban sociology.

The course's gravitational center was the "Everyday Section," drawn by hand at full scale to depict some of the students' houses. Providence was an ideal test-bed, since most of these houses were low-rise buildings from the late eighteenth, the

FIGURE 1.4.1 A 2006 installation of the annual Live Project by RISD first year architecture students.

nineteenth and the early to mid-twentieth century, often in timber. Every example had been retrofitted, a palimpsest of construction history.

Deploying empirical method

Teaching in a Live Projects context draws upon a different set of skills and capacities than the simulation-based paradigms typical in architecture school. Its demand for common sense is a good antidote to the mystification of architecture as specialist knowledge. The experiences of teamwork and physical labor, and of quickly resolving complex, multivariable problems in a spatial context so that work can proceed, reinforce different ways of understanding architecture than the heroic loneliness of the traditional studio or the temporal disjunction of late-night CAD monkeying.

Likewise, construction technology teaching is usually remote from first-hand interpolation (or common sense) on site. Most textbooks depict conventionalized examples from "standard practice" (which, as we all know, is only a rough average of the ad hoc variations on standard construction found at the job site). Even virtuosic renderings of construction techniques may not reveal the order of construction, tolerances, physical material properties, or interplay of labor at a detailed scale. They may gloss over the symbiosis of spatial, structural, environmental, and cultural significance that can be revealed even in modest projects when considered at full scale. To leverage the experience of full-scale realized work, building construction teaching should also interpolate between experience-based and intellect-based work and cultivate the ability to accrue, test, and extrapolate from empirical evidence rather than convention.

By celebrating both ingenuity and distributed authorship, construction teaching can reinforce an understanding of the word "architect" as a collective noun.

Ways of seeing

The kind of seeing at stake in teaching building construction within a Live Projects context is *deductive*. The gathering of appropriate visible evidence from which to interpolate invisible but decisive information underpinned the "Everyday Section," which began as a section cut through a window or door and was developed over several weeks to include foundation, floor, and roof junctures. This drawing was our method to compel students to conceptualize, stage, and architecturally evaluate a construction detail. It taught them to see dynamically, both into the building's past and towards a future as foreseen in the speculative projects which they developed in the latter portion of the semester. The semester's work was simply a Live Project run in reverse, from something existing in the world to a set of predictive documents.

X-ray vision

It was a revelation to most students that it is quite difficult to understand by whom and in what sequence the elements that comprise a building have been assembled. Their first assignment, the rendering of an aperture and standard exterior wall construction within their Everyday Sections, also required the inclusion of marginalia on the same drawing to describe how they thought construction might have been sequenced. The marginalia offered a document of and an aid to their interpolations from what could be seen.

Some students were ruthless in gathering information. Discreet and not so discreet holes were bored into gypsum board and plaster-on-lathe; photos were made using flashlights in the far reaches of attic eaves not seen since they were built. Much of what their sleuthing revealed was a surprise: the practice in the late eighteenth century of laying brick infill within timber construction for lateral stability and fireproofing; the resilience of balloon framing, which hung together from its integral supports as foundations bowed and distended beneath it; forgotten wall cavities for window counterweights and concealed shutters precisely configured in triple-wythe brick walls.

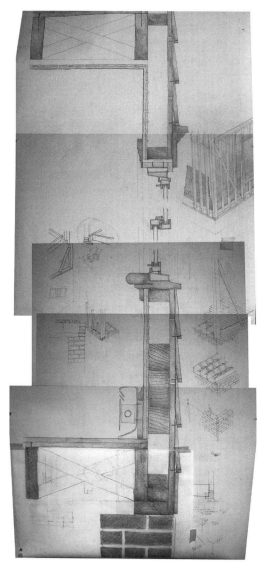

FIGURE 1.4.2 "Everyday Section" studying a balloon frame house partially infilled with brick. Note marginalia.

These searches produced very different kinds of drawings than those to be found in modern construction books. Drawn freehand in pencil or pastel, with each juncture indicated by two lines to denote where one element ended and the next began, the sections ghosted what lay behind or in front. Indicating the direction in which fasteners were inserted forced consideration of order of construction. The discovery of wooden shims which mediated between casework and envelope meant

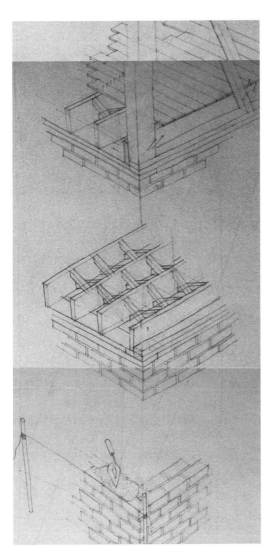

FIGURE 1.4.3 Marginalia on "Everyday Section."

the different grades of wood used had to be denoted in drawing according to the roles they played – from precise finished surface to blocking never intended to be seen.

By picking apart their buildings and rebuilding them through the process of drawing at full scale, the students learned how to see through matter and across time to the moment when the building had been put together. It is no coincidence that the identification of the built environment as fulcrum between its multiple authors and its even larger user group reiterates the conception and execution of Live Projects.

Rules and exceptions

The course also addressed the misconception among architecture students that the detail is either a singular moment to be celebrated (if not fetishized) or a banal expedience that best remains invisible. In both cases, construction and material are conflated with finish surface and the negotiation between visible and invisible that determines spatial expression is not recognized. A romanticized idea of the "tectonic" suppresses the fact that all construction types comprise rules and exceptions within which the architect has to decide what is expressed or repressed. These insights expanded upon the design/build portions of Live Project exercises: limited by skill and timeframe, design/build projects struggle to achieve the complexity of professionally built architecture. Nonetheless, they always make apparent that construction expression is much more than expedience.

In order to differentiate "standard" construction practice from ingenuity, virtuosity, or simple variation, the students were asked to study historical documents culled from online sources, such as the US Historical Building Survey, period construction handbooks in the library, and comparisons of Everyday Sections across the class. In analyzing this information they also mapped the sources of the materials used and tracked the off-site and on-site processes that had allowed these materials to be used in the final construction.

The benefits of this exercise were manifold. It allowed students to understand the process of construction detailing and realization as a symbiosis between the repetitive and the exceptional, relative to the spatial and volumetric consequences of each. It created awareness of the history of labor and material within the built environment, and how to read its traces. It also drove home the fact that material and labor were recorded in the built environment with a level of complexity not fully accounted for in calculating "embodied energy."

Systems thinking

In *IBS*, the lesson of systems thinking was to recognize that buildings are in a physical state of dynamic equipoise. This counters the usual teleology in which the just-finished building represents a high point before inevitable decay. To explain structure and envelope as mediators between two systems, one determined by gravity and environment and the other by the desire for human inhabitation, we invited four guest lecturers: a preservationist, an engineer with a background in material science and chemistry, an environmental scientist, and an urban sociologist.

Cyclical, not linear

The built environment's dynamism is tangible in a Live Project context. A gust of wind, a change in relative humidity, or a regrouping of people on site has immediate consequences. Rather than resisting this dynamism, students were asked to take the system's changing parameters into account to create a more responsive and robust built environment. One example they found was the shrinking and

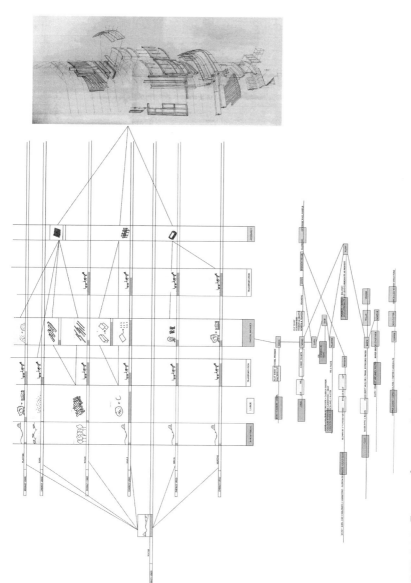

FIGURE 1.4.4 Excerpts from a study of a bay window in wood construction and the sources of its plaster and lathe *c.* 1890.

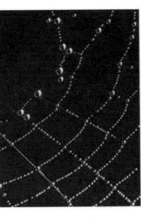

Weep Hole: A hole which allows for drainage of entrapped water from masonry or glazing structures.
Weep Screed: Tool used to drain moisture from concrete.

Weep hole: Small holes provided in the sill section of a sash to allow water or condensation to escape, and that might otherwise accumulate in a window sill; drainage opening in retaining wall;

Weep holes are designed to drain out any water that seeps through the brick or mortar. The only problem is that 95% of the time, as the brick wall is built, the excess mortar falls down the back wall and covers them up.

A weep hole is a bearing relief hole, and is intentionally placed on water pumps as an early indicator Also, check the lowest course of bricks for the presence of "weep holes" about every fourth mortar joint. of internal failure. Once a weep hole begins leaking, the damage inside is already done.

Cohesion causes water to form drops, surface tension causes them to be nearly spherical, and adhesion keeps the drops in place.

Adhesion is the tendency of certain dissimiliar molecules to cling together due to attractive forces.

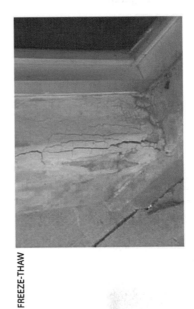

FREEZE-THAW

FIGURE 1.4.5 Scavenger hunt, adhesion and cohesion in building pathologies.

swelling of wood that caused constant recalibration within the intercut light-gauge balloon frame. Another was a forensic scavenger hunt for evidence, in construction materials, of the hydrological cycle in the built fabric along Providence's steeply sloping East Side.

The course also considered the city's cyclical growth and metabolism. Because the buildings we studied all represented different moments in Providence's urban history we could deduce such reciprocities as how the prevailing wind blowing across the city's coal-dust-powered electrical plant had determined what was built, and where.

Architects have to eat

The semester was divided between deductive (the Everyday Section) and speculative work, the "Not So Everyday." Between the two was an exercise entitled "Architects have to eat."

The exercise is simple: students map a communal meal they cook, from shopping and transportation through eating and cleanup, as a flow of locations, timing, resources, actors, and materials, in analogy to the building site choreography. The outcomes – which in several cases documented multiple trips to the wine store – reflected the labor/material interaction fundamental to construction.

Not so everyday

The touchstone for the students' internalization of our subject matter, we believed, was their ability to use it creatively. In the final four weeks of the semester they

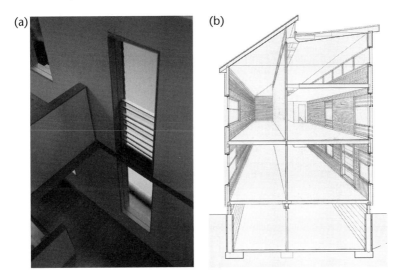

FIGURE 1.4.6 Final projects for an eighteenth- and nineteenth-century timber house.

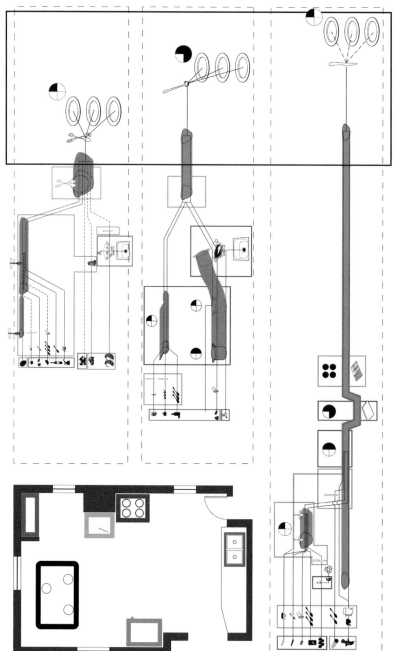

FIGURE 1.4.7 Kitchen plan and cooking diagram.

defined an architectural and spatial idea around which to develop a construction-based intervention into the building they had studied in their Everyday Sections. The projects demonstrated a high level of understanding and ability. We could even test their investment in distributed authorship, if unwittingly: students chose to be graded either individually or in the context of their group work. Interestingly, the strongest student work was done by those groups that elected to be evaluated together. They had understood that their individual efforts had become inextricable from one another.

Conclusions

Since I left architectural teaching behind in favor of Sustainability Management I have had the opportunity to observe the frequency of Live Projects in other professional courses of study. The alacrity with which students embrace the distribution of responsibilities throughout the group stands in sharp contrast to the fears about loss of self-expression and autonomy that can often cripple architectural students engaged in Live Projects. This normalized relationship to one's own production and to identifying ultimate aims that everyone's contributions serve seems the larger lesson to be learned here. Distributed authorship is not only a fact of architectural production but also a safe haven which architectural Live Projects can support and cultivate.

1.5

CO-AUTHORING A LIVE PROJECT MANIFESTO

Harriet Harriss

Engaging the thinker-practitioner

Most architecture manifestos fall into two categories: those that ascribe aesthetics and those that agitate ideologically. This chapter concerns the latter. Drafted in a workshop session at the 2012 *Architecture 'Live Project' Pedagogy* symposium at Oxford Brookes University, the Live Project Manifesto seeks to consolidate a range of Live Project educator and student narratives into something cohesive that could form the basis of a tentative assessment framework.

From the Latin *manus* (hand) and *festus* (from *fendo*, to dash against), a manifesto appears to be the ideal vehicle for facilitating curricula insurrection. Manifestos offer the chance to engage the 'thinker-practitioner' (Danchev 2011), requiring them to express practical as well as philosophical sagacity. Many renowned architects have sequestered the manifesto. Jencks and Kropof's *Theories and Manifestoes of Contemporary Architecture* (2006) contains no fewer than 121 such declarations, yet none of them address architectural education. According to Mark Wigley – Dean of Columbia University's Graduate School of Architecture – many architecture manifestos are 'concerned with change yet operate independent of their consequences' (Wigley in Buckley 2013; cited in Holt and Looby 2011). In contrast, the Live Project educator manifesto is every bit concerned with consequences: consequences founded upon 'tested' ideas; consequences that positively impact on the learner/collaborator; consequences that define the context in which the Live Project takes place.

Although not intended as a diatribe, the manifesto challenges the conditions under which architectural education currently takes place and consequently how we then assess students' ability to develop and act upon 'architectural' expertise. So how and why is a manifesto the best model for capturing this?

Interesting, erudite, but mostly just relevant

After posting his own education manifesto on his Cooper Union blog, educator and practitioner Lebbeus Woods concluded that the lack of any online responses or 'objections' indicated that the manifesto was either considered 'boring' or insufficiently 'controversial', or that 'readers don't care about architectural education' (Woods 2011). Subsequently, one might deduce from this that an education manifesto should simply be both interesting and contrary – presumably by merely challenging the established ways of doing things. However, to conflate an indifference towards the author and his views with an indifference towards architectural curricula seems a conceit that fails to consider the importance of the relationship between the manifesto and the milieu – that the most conspicuous if not successful manifestos (from the US Declaration of Independence to the *Futurist Manifesto*) are those that either are collectively authored and/or directly address collective concerns. Since the Live Project workshop embodied all of these qualifying characteristics, the manifesto seemed the most apt of conventions to attempt to decalcify architectural curricula.

Death, deferral, or radical pedagogy

As Beatriz Colomina argues, radical pedagogy needs to be understood as a type of radical architectural practice in its own right (Colomina 2012). She also identifies that this 'radical' challenge to the established foundations of architectural education has been 'surprisingly neglected in recent years, yet was a normative part of postwar thinking', and that instead schools (and their contents) have become 'timid'. Jeremy Till takes this one step further in using grave terms to surmise the 'slow death' of 'lifeless pedagogy' within UK architectural education (Till 2012: 4, 6). Whether terminal or timid, what is apparent is that there are few if any pedagogic pioneers within today's architecture schools. Instead, we seem inclined to defer the opportunity to innovate to others. A case in point concerns Donald Schön's 'reflective practitioner' (Schön 1987). His oft-cited text extolled the virtues of design studio as an exemplary practice-meets-academy learning environment. Schön was neither architect nor educator but in fact a management consultant. That someone outside architectural education should prove so successful in articulating the pedagogic integrity of architecture curricula makes the urgency and significance of an architect voice defining – rather than deferring – the territory to others even more acute. What happened in the Live Project workshop involved a clawing back of some of this territory. For example, since Live Projects take place off-campus they mount a direct challenge to Schön's idée fixe that 'reflection' is design studio-dependent. Instead, what Live Projects offer is more than the reflection-in-action and reflection-on-action that can be achieved arguably more effectively within the real-time challenges of a Live Project space than a design studio. What they also offer the student is the chance to reflect back on their experience of learning architecture within an institution and to question its meaning, relevance, and

FIGURE 1.5.1 A Live Project soaking: architecture student Will Harrison demonstrates Pascal's principle of fluid mechanics using a water balloon.

(social) value. In doing this, Live Projects bravely 'radicalize' architecture pedagogy by reviving dying architectural curricula and reversing their terminal decline.

The Live Project Manifesto

As the education philosopher Robin Barrow argues, radical action concerns fundamental change. Change in itself is neither good nor bad. What matters instead is what we want to change and how we intend to do it (Barrow 2011). The manifesto tenets captured are radical not just because they agitate established pedagogy, as illustrated in the Schön scenario, but because they propose fledgling forms of tested-in-practice pedagogy. As sixteenth-century physician Blaise Pascal's fluid mechanics experiment proved, when pressure is exerted against an incompressible fluid, the pressure is transmitted equally in all directions (Bloomfield 2006). Similarly, the principles outlined in the Live Project educators' manifesto exert pressure in the same way – not by presenting an inert list of assessment tick boxes that perpetuate established pedagogies, but by offering criteria for measuring Live Project efficacy that are precipitated by bespoke contexts and new forms of architectural knowledge and expertise. The tenets are outlined below.

'Respond to the pressing need'

To what extent do the proposed/realized design 'solutions' (whether brief, report, or building) reflect the needs of either the situation they seek to address and/or the students' need to learn from it? Prioritizing a Live Project's fit-for-purpose outcomes engenders responsibility among the students. It also requires that students work effectively with the community to define the need and to co-create possible solutions.

'Reward successful failure'

As one educator at the Live Project Symposium (2012) argued, 'failure can be successful'. Learning from failure is widely acknowledged as a skill that enables students to learn more effectively and predisposes them to better manage future crises – an invaluable skill in uncertain times (Pearson and Clair 1998). Subsequently, we should assess, when things go wrong, how successful the students are at using the failure to find alternative solutions or to demonstrate that they had learned from it.

'Measure social impact'

Architects are largely preoccupied with material rather than social outcomes. Yet underlying social issues are often hard to serve. Live Projects' success should involve post-completion visits and might also involve assessment and/or management beyond the constraints of individual academic years. Since the Social Impact Assessment (SIA) is understood to 'identify the future consequences of current or proposed actions' (Becker 1997: 2), post-occupancy work can involve speculations as well as observations, exercises that encourage students to anticipate or consider 'the way in which people work, play, relate to one another, organize to meet their needs' (ibid.). Subsequently, educators should distribute the points at which we assess students over a broader timeline to more effectively measure lasting social impact and to consider evidence for efficacy beyond the point of construction completion.

'(Re)define what is valuable'

Enabling students to participate in determining what should be assessed offers a highly effective strategy for assessment buy-in (Boud et al. 1999) in terms of peer learning and the integration of new knowledge and ideas. In addition, as some educators at the Live Project Symposium pointed out, Live Projects help students to recognize not only 'the value of their own skills and knowledge and that of others' but also 'the value of their own labour' – a advantageous awareness in recession-strapped times. Consequently, educators should collectively determine what students want to achieve in terms of knowledge, skills, and experience, and measure performance relative to mutually agreed goals.

'Reward the missing skills'

Although assessing prior learning is not a new idea (Knapp 1977) it is not something we seem particularly geared towards within architecture teaching. Students bring a range of skills to bear that can prove invaluable to Live Project participation and processes, yet these skills are not easy to reward within the established RIBA/ARB or NAAB criteria. Subsequently, recognizing and rewarding students' maverick expertise is one way to increase and support diversification in both learning methods and student profile. This requires us to assess skills that the students bring and apply within Live Projects, not just those they learn on the job.

'Engender criticality, complexity, conflict'

According to Stanislav Roudavski, 'critical pedagogies are effective for such preparations because they encourage conflict as a strategy that is capable of sustaining multiple alternatives' (Roudavski 2012). As one workshop group contended, 'LP's help students to assume a critical and reflective position – one that is open to criticism, open to intervention from people who are not of the same academic culture.' Subsequently, students exposed to complexity and conflict can become more capable problem-solvers, collaborators, strategists, and resource managers. Live Project assessments should therefore engender and reward students' ability to manage complexity and embrace criticality as a means to locate or propose alternative strategies.

Conclusions

These six tenets provide a transposable, deployable tool for Live Project educators in the field of architecture and beyond, in that they support educational experiences designed to facilitate authentic and measurable learning that matters. They can be used to inform students' assessment criteria as a means to measure both student and community gains. They contain a built-in flexibility to adapt and respond to change through their willingness to embrace a process of 'live' co-authorship in defining a good project, relative to both student and civic outcome. These tenets are informed by the wealth of case studies featured elsewhere in this book. Yet all of these case studies are unique, providing further evidence that Live Projects are a resilient and adaptable pedagogy.

One potential criticism is that co-authoring a manifesto of 'best practice' as a means to inform a set of shared assessment criteria diminishes the acclaimed adaptability of Live Projects to respond to emergent circumstances. However, this manifesto aims to acknowledge rather than impose a way of teaching and learning about architecture that is effective *because* it is nimble, tenacious, and responsive. As Marinetti argued in his 1909 *Futurist Manifesto*, 'literature' should not be overtaken by progress; rather, it should 'absorb' progress in its evolution to allow our 'instinctive' nature to explode, in true fluid mechanics fashion.

Subsequently, this manifesto proposes a way of measuring learning that perpetuates the nimble, tenacious, and responsive qualities that Live Projects espouse.

References

Barrow, R. (2011). *Radical Education: A Critique of Freeschooling and Deschooling*, vol. 7. Routledge.

Becker, H.A. (1997). *Social Impact Assessment: Method and Experience in Europe, North America and the Developing World*. UCL Press.

Bloomfield, L. (2006). *How Things Work: The Physics of Everyday Life*, 3rd edn. John Wiley & Sons.

Boud, D., Cohen, R., and Sampson, J. (1999). 'Peer Learning and Assessment'. *Assessment & Evaluation in Higher Education*, 24(4): 413–426.

Buckley, C. (ed.) (2013). *After the Manifesto*. GSAPP/T6 Ediciones.

Colomina, B., with Choi, E., Gonzalez Galan, I., & Meister, A.-M. (2012). 'Radical Pedagogies in Architectural Education'. *Architectural Review*, 28 September. Available online at: http://www.architectural-review.com/essays/radical-pedagogies-in-architectural-education/8636066.article Accessed January 2014.

Danchev, A. (ed.) (2011). *100 Artists' Manifestos: From the Futurists to the Stuckists*. Penguin.

Holt, M. and Looby, M. (2011). 'What Happened to the Architectural Manifesto?' *Domus Magazine*, 1 December.

Jencks, C., and Kropof, K. (2006). *Theories and Manifestoes of Contemporary Architecture*. Wiley-Academy.

Knapp, J. (1977). *Assessing Prior Learning: A CAEL Handbook*. Cooperative Assessment of Experiential Learning.

Pearson, C.M., and Clair, J.A. (1998). 'Reframing Crisis Management'. *Academy of Management Review*, 23(1): 59–76.

Schön, Donald, A. (1987). *Educating the Reflective Practitioner*. Jossey-Bass.

Till, J. (2012). *Architecture Depends*. MIT Press.

Woods, L. (2011). 'Manifesto: The Reality of Ideals'. Available online at: http: lebbeuswoods.wordpress.com/2011/06/06/manifesto-the-reality-of-ideals/Accessed January 2014.

PART II

The question of assessment

2.1

WORKING MARGINS, DRAWING LINES

David Gloster

Definitions

A consideration of the fit of Live Projects in relation to professional bodies' requirements for schools of architecture requires establishing where the margins of acceptability for curricular activity lie and suggests narrowing our definitions of Live Projects to something manageable enough to disagree over. For example:

1. **Developmental/analogous.** The project is small-scale, providing focus and place for users whose development needs are unattractive to conventional professional arrangements; the key conversation is user–designer, the designer frequently operating as constructor.
2. **Self-conceived/self-built.** The project is medium-scale and provides permanent habitation, but develops outside constraints of consistency and design guidance offered by a professional team; the key conversation is user–subcontractor, the user directing construction.
3. **Enabling/spontaneous.** The project addresses primary human needs developing from conflict or natural disaster; the requirement is for fast-tracked volume provision outside precepts of concept and detailed design development.
4. **Constructional/remnant.** The project constructs a fragment of a design proposal using those authentic materials intended for more complete execution, but with attitudes to detail that may not treat issues of habitation, servicing, etc.
5. **Interstitial/interventionist.** The project works as literal or metaphorical land grab, using low(-ish) technology for short-term occupation of the city; this offers political markers for concerns about vacancy, dereliction, or lack of investment.

Let's assume this list is faulty and incomplete, but useful as a basic taxonomy. We may then situate the Live Project in the architectural/academic canon, asking why this vehicle is durable enough to be persistently reviewed. The key determinant of the Live Project's popularity is simple: it provides accessibility to high(-ish) and low/no design solutions suggestive of a guerilla ethic, processes largely sidestepped. So, it is unsurprising that those clustered around the production of architecture are drawn to Live Projects; they provide architects with a channel to making something useful *extra muris* of normative professionalized procedures.

Other ways

A *frisson* permeates current conversations about the architect's role, reflected in Jeremy Till's *Spatial Agency: Other Ways of Doing Architecture* (Till 2011). This book is intelligent, well-structured, and coherent; it summarizes 50 years of affirmative action by commentators, artists, architects, and students dodging the straitjackets of an increasingly corporate profession. It is a *Whole Earth Catalog*[1] of seized opportunities, providing 'tools to work within – or despite of – prevalent political systems. . . [to] take an extremely politicised stance and radically oppose, resist, and refuse to work within frameworks . . . set by the neo-liberal economy' (Till 2011: 79).

It is hard to disagree with the book's sentiments, to dispute its utility in recession, or suggest that the strategies described give anything but hope to graduates who feel they have been disadvantaged by the chronological accident of their birth. Critically, it premiates the value of Live Projects. However, there are problems with the narrative, and some unease about Live Projects themselves.

Clarification and explanation are first needed. It has been suggested that 'Live Projects sit outside . . . the architecture curriculum set out by the . . . Royal Institute of British Architects . . . this means they are not "accredited" learning' (Harriss 2012: introductory notes). As this statement gets any number of deep-lunged hares running, it is worth probing why the Live Project could be characterized as an academic outsider, questioning where the margins of academic work reside – and who actually draws them.

The RIBA

The uneasy relationship between what is viewed as admissible evidence welcomed by RIBA validation – work *inside* the margins – and initiatives located 'outside' the validation system is founded on misconceptions that validation sets censorial parameters inhibiting restructuration of the architect's role. The grim RIBA Outline Syllabus (RIBA 1998) appears to prescribe curricular content. While redundant after 2003, when validation criteria were offered for interpretation by schools, its successor, *Tomorrow's Architect* (RIBA 2003), consolidated a sense that the RIBA had views about what was, or was *not*, appropriate activity for a student of architecture.

Tomorrow's Architect refers to 'design projects . . . [which] demonstrate the graduate's ability in the integrated design of complex buildings' (ibid.: 38). This fails to differentiate between educating students in the complex, interactive themes that develop a reflective architect, and the finite tasks of practice. Schools should not be a microcosm of normative practice but an explosive catalyst for students to progress the theories and practice of architecture. To suggest that 'integrated design' is within the grasp of even the brightest student misses the point: 'integrated' work is produced by a design *team*, and cannot be a feasible expectation of single graduates. Lack of comprehensiveness and integration in a completed construction project *is* unforgiveable, but the capacity of open academic ideas to pique debate and advance knowledge is fundamental to education. Piranesi's theatricality and multiple viewpoints outweigh demands on his work for completeness; it is the *absence* of the whole that renders his folio delicious. Room is left for ambiguity and interpretation.

Interpretation is critical to understanding validation; no approach to architecture education is considered by the RIBA as outside the margins providing that the school justifies its approach in a credible academic position statement and mapping document (RIBA 2011: 22) and demonstrates, through students' work, an honouring of intentions. RIBA validation is not a procedural panopticon from which to scrutinize schools or caution dissenters, instead giving universities responsibility for developing that 'diverse, engaging, rigorous, and intelligent raft of schools of architecture, each clearly distinguished from the other by defined academic objectives and a sense of the individual identity of their courses and qualifications' (ibid.: 49) the RIBA wishes to develop. So Live Projects fall comfortably within 'the margins'; no line call needed.

The city

Critically, the Live Project challenges European precepts of permanence. Architecture's collective iconography defines our cities; the constructs Rossi referred to in *The Architecture of the City* as 'urban artifacts' remain a visual shorthand for understanding London, Paris, Moscow, New York, Rome – even the Emirates.

> Permanences present two aspects; on the one hand, they can be considered as propelling elements, on the other, as pathological elements. Artifacts either enable us to see the city in its totality, or they appear as a series of isolated elements that we can link only tenuously to an urban system ... the physical form of the past has assumed different functions and has continued to function, conditioning the urban area in which it stands, and continuing to constitute an important urban focus.
>
> *(Rossi 1982: 59)*

Yet the prevailing trend is of less rooted, informal settlement located at the threshold of the planned city but possessing little of the nobility, craft, and tectonic integrity permeating Rossi's account of an acceptable urbanism. The western sensibility of the Live Project unconsciously stages a reality well known to the morphing *favelas* of Lima or Mumbai. Here the appropriation of civic space unconsciously echoes Lefebvre, born from visceral needs for shelter and access to work/water.

Vivid, sometimes lurid, illustrations from Montreal and Christchurch suggest that frustration with policies whereby private interests control social life to maximize profit is not limited to the disenfranchised crowds in Tahrir and Syntagma Squares. The Maple Spring unfolding in French-Canadian cities and the stalling of earthquake reconstruction in New Zealand are both eerily absent from western media. These events correspond closely to the Greek debt crisis and the Bush administration's lack of interest in New Orleans after Hurricane Katrina hit in August 2005; if conditions of 'emergency' are permanently embedded in popular consciousness it is easier for governments to engender an alleviated normality skewed by imperatives of crisis.

Resistive models

Within education there is similar ferment when opposing the metaphor of a 'school without windows' (Brown 2012); a mixed learning community for students of architecture in partnership with their engineering peer group may provide a useful baseline to evaluate our general perspectives on multiple authorship. This concept of an 'aesthetic of the variable in a self-managing community' (Denicke-Polcher and Khonsari 2012) is seductive, and resurrects the collaborative networks reconfiguring the commissioning of structures and buildings envisaged by Lewis Mumford. Mumford is relevant: in framing one of few viable proposals for sustainable regional development capable of co-habiting with American capitalism, he posits a model resistive to cultural congruence and capable of succeeding through stealth.

> The adaptation of a culture to a particular environment is a long, complicated process; a full-blown regional characteristic is the last to emerge ... regional forms are those which most closely meet the actual conditions of life, and which most fully succeed in making a people feel at home in their environment; they do not merely utilise the soil, but they reflect the current conditions of culture in the region.
>
> *(Mumford 1967: 29–30)*

Live projects working beneath the educational radar encourage conspiracies of trust between collaborators, to resolve those tensions in the professional role potentially capable of grounding promising ideas. Consideration of these tactics leads seamlessly into considering how Live Project offices situated on campus may develop built prototypes for the revival of shared space. If the notion can be established that urban open space is available to all and its use not limited by social demographic or time, this principle may be extended into the streets and parks of the city, with rights of access embedded in the citizenry. While the control and sanitization of American civic space appears now as a given, it is because a consensus presumptuously emerged that more inclusive use of the city was *over* the margin.

The vitality of affirmative action leading to constructed projects outside current procurement garottes is uplifting. The political ethos of Live Project work reminds us that twentieth-century Modernism was laced with themes of social redemption and equality. Building on a motherlode of ethical action, the twenty-first-century graduate must be a cybersmart fleet fox, a mini-Vitruvian, at home in the editing suite, workshop, or site. The vivacious and intriguing concept before us, therefore, is how to equip the Live Project with the centrality, urgency, and soul-stirring character of a Goya painting, to recommend it as a model for guerilla practice, teaching, and fabrication transferable to the streets.

Doing better

So we need to be frank about limitations in the Live Project vehicle and ask whether it fulfils enough requirements to displace other models or continue as an intriguing curricular supplement.

> We are none of us so good architects as to be able to habitually work beneath our strength, and yet there is not a building that I know of, lately raised, wherein it is not sufficiently evident that neither architect nor builder has done his best . . . ours has as constantly the look of money's worth, of a stopping short wherever and whenever we can, of a lazy compliance with low conditions; never of a fair putting forth of our strength . . . it is not a question of doing more, but of doing better.
>
> *(Ruskin 1989: 21)*

While Ruskin may not be an obvious source from which to critique the Live Project, his architecture *versus* building argument remains as relevant now as it was to the mid nineteenth century. Referring back to the informal city, the prevailing trend in global construction is for *building*: building high, wide, and quickly, with the intention of enclosing as much volume as possible for least expenditure of time and money. As the informal city grows, it is at the expense of those historical urban centres that define the iconography of the city/region. This is not an argument for perpetuating the relational opposition of soaring cathedral/ground-hugging hovel that defined medieval Europe, but it suggests that we have to define dignifying strategies to make sense of the pyroclastic flow of informality.

Beautiful stuff

Such strategies require re-engagement with priorities that there is a subtle suggestion to relegate.

> Beauty has been used too often as an excuse to retreat from some of the more contested areas of contemporary life, as if a timeless sense of beauty will lift us from our daily grind . . . the connection between beauty and betterment is so taken for granted that the motivation to make the world a better place is

surreptitiously replaced with the more simple, and more controllable, motivation of making beautiful stuff.

(Awan et al. 2011: 37)

This is a clever enough argument to start a scrap with, but with flaws too obvious to
pass over. Firstly, it is glib to suggest that poverty lived in the shadow of the cathedral
(to obliquely reference Vicente Ibanez's book (Ibanez 2006)) is less grinding than
in any less privileged physical context. Secondly, a 'timeless sense of beauty' is not
an undesirable quality; only the mean-minded would dismiss it as such. Thirdly,
connection between beauty and betterment fuelled little built work during the past
50 years; for every so-called icon there has been a weak wash of poorly conceived
background work keenly proclaiming the modesty of its values. Finally, it is because
the production of 'beautiful stuff' is *not* 'simple' that makes it rare, and all the more
important when architecture does project such qualities. We would be reluctant to
probe the simplicity/controllability theorem in relation to Leonardo's *Leda and the
Swan* or Turner's seascapes; why does architecture constitute a different case, better
suited to this test?

More is more

So, let's draw together the divergent beauty/authenticity axes and ask those involved
with the Live Project to consider a further five points for inclusion in their work.

1. **A project may aspire to (or indeed communicate) a 'timeless sense of
   beauty'**; this does not disqualify it from offering authentic tools to 'radically
   oppose, resist, and refuse to work within . . . neo-liberal frameworks' (Till 2011:
   79).
2. The design parameters for Live Projects may also **develop correspondence
   with theoretical considerations of aesthetics drawn from architectural
   historiography**; the utility of the project, and its socio-political impact or
   perceived oppositional value, are only partial answers to design problems.
3. Found sites should not presuppose the unconsidered use of found materials, even
   if these are economically attractive; the Live Project should **zealously pursue
   the idea of tectonic craft** in its execution.
4. The project should both support narrative specific to the temporal point at
   which it is produced, and **communicate expectations of an experiential
   and operational value beyond the immediate period of execution.**
5. The Live Project is a viable avenue of investigation, securely situated within the
   professional validation envelope; the diversity of professional activity suggests it
   as **one of a series of educational models** contributing to the emergence of
   graduates as versatile problem solvers.

This five-point plan neither diminishes Live Projects nor denies practical and
intellectual skills developed from immersion in such initiatives. What it questions

is how we distinguish architecture from building, and why any reductivism in our discipline is neither desirable nor practical. The attributes required of successful projects mean the designer tackles *more* rather than fewer issues; a properly holistic resolution of all intellectual activity constituting design is tougher than it was 30 years ago. The profession might be reminded of this when offering any critique of graduate employability. The difficulty architecture faces rests with the fact that there are architects who are neither skilled, persuasive, nor willing designers – despite protestations to the contrary. While 'other ways of doing architecture' are genuinely welcomed, the larger question of how students fathom the depth of what design fully constitutes remains perplexing. In engaging with the margins it may be helpful to recall where the lines lie, and what values these need to reflect.

Note

1 Stewart Brand's self-published revival (in 1968) of the American nineteenth-century mail order catalogue for the Microbus generation who, post-Altamont, saw back to the land as having fresh appeal.

References

Awan, N., Schneider, T., and Till, J. (2011). *Spatial Agency: Other Ways of Doing Architecture*. Routledge.

Brand, S. (ed.) (1968). *Whole Earth Catalog*. Whole Earth Catalog.

Brown, A. (2012). 'Interdisciplinary Live Project Studio'. Paper given at Live Projects Pedagogy International Symposium, Oxford, 25 May 2012.

Denicke-Polcher, S. and Khonsari, T. (2012). 'Architecture of Multiple Authorship'. Paper given at Live Projects Pedagogy International Symposium, Oxford, 25 May 2012.

Ibanez, V. B. (2006). *The Shadow of the Cathedral*. Reprint of 1919 edition. BiblioBazaar.

James, W. (2008). *Pragmatism: A New Name for Some Old Ways of Thinking* (aphorism 5: lecture 6). Reprint of 1907 edition. Arc Manor.

Mumford, L. (1967). *The South in Architecture: The Dancy Lectures Alabama College 1941*. Reprint of 1941 edition. Da Capo.

Harriss, H. (2012). 'Live Projects Pedagogy International Symposium, Paper Submission Guidelines'. Oxford Brookes University.

Rossi, A. (1982). *The Architecture of the City*. Reprint of 1966 edition. MIT Press.

Royal Institute of British Architects (1998). *Outline Syllabus*. RIBA Enterprises Ltd.

Royal Institute of British Architects (2003). *Tomorrow's Architect*. RIBA Enterprises Ltd.

Royal Institute of British Architects (2011). *RIBA Procedures for Validation and Validation Criteria for UK and International Courses and Examinations in Architecture*. RIBA Education.

Ruskin, J. (1989). *The Seven Lamps of Architecture (The Lamp of Sacrifice)*. Reprint of 1880 second edition (first edition 1849). Dover Publications.

2.2

THE NAAB LIVE PROJECT PARADIGM

Christine Theodoropoulos

Live Projects are project-based learning experiences that engage students in applied architectural practice. They are commonplace in US schools of architecture and widely accepted by educators and practitioners as an effective means for achieving learning outcomes that meet the conditions of accreditation defined by the National Architectural Accrediting Board (NAAB). The merits of Live Project learning have been extensively promoted through national awards programs sponsored by the Association of Collegiate Schools of Architecture (ACSA) – the organization of schools offering accredited programs – and the National Council of Architectural Registration Boards (NCARB) – the organization that establishes criteria for professional licensure. The NCARB prize for Creative Integration of Practice and Education in the Academy, awarded to accredited programs between 2001 and 2011, recognized many Live Projects for their successful involvement of practicing architects in the education of future architects (*NCARB Prize Program 2001–2011*). The ACSA's annual awards program includes the Collaborative Practice Award for school-based community outreach programs, and the Design-Build Award for school-based design/build projects, both with a history of bestowing awards for Live Project achievements (*ASCA Collaborative Practice Award*; *ASCA Collaborative Practice Award*).

The path to architectural licensure

For most US-educated architects the path to architectural licensure includes two educational phases: completion of a degree program accredited by the NAAB and completion of an Intern Development Program required for certification by the National Council of Architectural Registration Boards (NCARB) (n.a. 2009; *NCARB Intern Development Program*). The NAAB evaluates schools' achievement of student performance criteria by sending visiting teams to schools where they examine work produced by students. The NCARB evaluates interns' achievement of experience requirements through supervisor or mentor reporting. In recent years NCARB revised its Intern Development Program to include relevant experience students gain in conjunction with academic programs in schools. As a result, students can use experience gained in Live Projects offered by community-service design organizations affiliated with schools to meet internship requirements if they participate in ways that do not also fulfill academic requirements for their accredited degree program, usually as employees or volunteer interns. NCARB also recognizes a number of Live Project-intensive, post-professional advanced degree programs as contributing elective experience hours.

Most schools using Live Projects to fulfill accreditation criteria balance live and simulated activities within the curriculum. Learning to produce architecture in real-world conditions through Live Projects is useful for meeting many student performance criteria required for accreditation, especially those associated with design implementation and professional responsibilities, but the challenges inherent in Live Projects can sometimes make it difficult to meet learning objectives consistently. In simulated projects instructors can tailor the project scope and design process to ensure that students acquire the specific knowledge and abilities they are expected to demonstrate to accreditation reviewers. In Live Projects, project constraints and the changing needs of external partners or stakeholders whose priorities differ from the educational objectives of the program can affect learning outcomes. Instructors who teach Live Projects that meet accreditation standards take great care to select projects and partners that support learning objectives. They plan student experience to meet specific performance criteria using pedagogical approaches that, in many ways, resemble the control faculty exercise when teaching simulated projects. Alternatively, at many schools, Live Projects are offered outside of the accredited curricular requirements as elective options for interested students, with freedom to pursue learning that varies according to the type of project or role assumed by the student.

Accreditation challenges

Given the diversity of Live Project types and accreditation intents, it is difficult to generalize about accreditation issues. Schools offering Live Projects as part of an accredited program confront challenges that pose questions. Are there limitations to a visiting team's ability to evaluate Live Projects and is there a need for improvement in how schools present and how teams assess learning outcomes? Is confirmation of individual student learning difficult because Live Projects are usually collaborative efforts, rather than individual efforts? Is confirmation of specific subject area knowledge difficult because Live Projects are integrated activities rather than specialized activities? Do Live Projects, practically constrained by time, cost, or constructability, lack sufficient complexity for students to acquire the skills they need to be competent building designers? Do instructors, who are pressured to meet external demands for project deliverables, exercise too much control over student work, thereby reducing opportunities for students to learn through self-directed exploration or by making mistakes? Can Live Projects be too time-consuming and inefficient to include in demanding professional curricula without negatively impacting learning in other areas? Is the amount of time students spend on the physical construction of some types of Live Projects more appropriate preparation for careers in the building trades rather than careers as architects?

These questions are best addressed by schools rather than accrediting bodies. The NAAB's approach to evaluating student performance criteria is based on the principle that accreditation is for the purpose of ensuring quality through the development and assessment of standards without presuming to standardize how schools choose to meet them (*Conditions for Accreditation for Professional Degree Programs in Architecture*). This supports diversity in architectural education and encourages schools to develop programs that leverage their unique identities and missions. It means that a school can propose an accredited curriculum in which all learning takes place through Live Projects without encountering any intended obstacles or negative bias from the NAAB. It also means that the NAAB should not create a condition of accreditation that requires schools to include Live Projects in their programs. In the US context of professional licensure this is appropriate, because students who do not engage in Live Projects in school have other opportunities to gain real-world experience through the Internship Development Program.

Maintaining a distinction between educational outcomes and the means to achieve them is essential if schools are to retain the flexibility that furthers opportunity to advance the quality of architectural education. The language of the NAAB Conditions, developed by the board using a process involving extensive outreach and consultation with organizations representing schools, students, architects, and architectural registration boards, occasionally lapses into requirements that can be seen to conflict with the flexibility intent, but ongoing dialog as conditions are revised, and as visiting teams are trained, tends to correct for this because of the consistency of the standards-without-standardization basis for assessment.

To better understand ways in which Live Projects can support accreditation, it is helpful to classify them into activity types and examine how they can be used to meet student performance criteria. Some common types are detailed below.

Temporary installations

Students gain experience exploring material, form, process, and meaning through hands-on, full-scale experimentation. There are relatively few external constraints other than those posed by a site – often located at the school. Project programs include furniture or exhibition structures as well as more open-ended spatial studies related to a conceptual theme or material. Learning objectives tend to focus on how design concepts are translated into material form, with an emphasis on tectonics and aesthetic expression. In recent years many of these installation-scale projects have focused on new technologies. Computational design and fabrication methods, applications of repurposed or recycled materials, and intelligent or sentient environments have been common themes.

Temporary installations often address aspects of student performance criteria in Realm A, defined by the NAAB as Critical Thinking and Representation. They may also contribute to, but are unlikely to fully meet, criteria in Realm B, Integrated Building Practices, Technical Skills and Knowledge. When schools present temporary installations to visiting teams they tend to focus on how these projects contribute to their program's creative culture. Visiting teams are more likely to reference this work in their discussion of conditions related to program identity and mission than cite installations as the primary location for meeting particular student performance criteria.

Shelter constructions

There is a long tradition of design-your-own-shelter projects that challenge students to address fundamental conditions of dwelling using minimal means. At the Frank Lloyd Wright School of Architecture and California Polytechnic State University the core curriculum includes assignments for students to design and construct shelters they will occupy, either for a day or for more extended periods (*Taliesin Student Shelters*). Learning objectives address site selection, structure, construction, and protection from the elements as well as programmatic requirements related to privacy, comfort, activity, experience, and identity. In recent years a popular, and often more technically rigorous, variation on the shelter project involves students in the design, construction and testing of emergency shelters. Several studios in schools of architecture have contributed to faculty research or participated in competitions with this focus.

The simple, yet comprehensive, nature of shelter projects make them an effective context for meeting activity-related learning outcomes, such as the ability to collaborate on interdisciplinary teams or the ability to use investigative skills. Shelter projects have the capacity to engage students in a short-term design/build activity that relates to a majority of student performance criteria, but because of their limited architectural scope these projects will not fully meet criteria that relate to the design of buildings, integration of technical systems, or the criteria defined in Realm C, Leadership and Practice, that address the responsibilities of architects related to project management, professional practice, or legal issues.

Small buildings

The design and construction of permanent dwellings and other small buildings for real clients is a longstanding hallmark of the Yale Building Project and the Rural Studio at Auburn. Both have provided students with an accessible, comprehensive design experience (based on the idea that teamwork, rather than individual work, is a valid and verifiable method to achieve educational outcomes) (Hayes 2007; *Rural Studio*). Many US schools of architecture offer students the opportunity to participate in design/build work; however, these opportunities are often elective rather than required and therefore do not receive the same scrutiny by accreditation teams as does required coursework.

Design/build projects that are integrated into an architecture curriculum tend to resemble the professional practice work students are preparing for and easily demonstrate achievement of accreditation learning objectives related to construction or systems integration as well as professional practice issues such as legal and economic constraints or client and community service. A number of these were recognized with the NCARB prize – clear validation that their value as education is recognized. Another notable competition is the biennial Solar Decathlon, sponsored by the US Department of Energy, in which schools design, construct, and measure the performance of solar-powered houses. Schools participating in the Solar Decathlon use these projects to showcase achievement across the curriculum, including comprehensive design ability (*US Department of Energy Solar Decathlon*).

The resources design/build projects require, and their scheduling needs (which can be difficult to align with an academic calendar), make it especially challenging for schools to involve every student in design/build work in a manner that consistently addresses specific student learning objectives. For this reason most design/build projects are presented as evidence of a school's learning culture and elective opportunities, rather than as meeting required student performance criteria.

School and community design partnerships

Although schools avoid competing with practicing architects for design commissions, there is a long tradition of designing for non-profit organizations and communities that cannot otherwise afford architects' services. At many schools these Live Project efforts are organized by community design centers affiliated with the university, such as the Tulane City Center, where faculty and students contribute to community-based organizations across New Orleans (*Tulane City Center*). Schools also partner with charitable organizations, such as Habitat for Humanity. Projects range from single buildings to urban design or regional planning. They are often funded through contracts with external partners and taught by faculty who are active practitioners.

As educational experiences, design partnership projects are celebrated nationally as exemplary contexts for architectural education that integrate numerous learning objectives while providing students with opportunities to serve communities. They have been recognized by numerous awards programs and contribute substantially to university regional identity. Accreditation teams view them as equal to simulated design projects when assessing student performance criteria. Although there are a number of examples of community design projects integrated into required courses or studios, much of this work occurs outside of the core accredited curriculum, where small groups of students participate as volunteers and paid interns or receive academic credit for elective studies or internships. As with design/build, it can be difficult for schools to rely on design partnership projects to consistently meet student performance criteria while maintaining the agility they need to best serve partnership interests.

Live-simulated hybrids

One of the most common and most flexible approaches to the use of Live Projects is a hybrid in which a real project is used as a vehicle for student learning and external partners participate with the understanding that they will benefit from their involvement in an educational process rather than receive an architectural service or product. Live-simulated hybrids are common to intermediate and advanced architecture studios. They balance the educational advantages of application with those of simulation. It is a pragmatic compromise that allows for creative exploration that would be difficult within the constraints of many Live Projects, yet engages students with clients who invite them to influence a project's future. The format of instruction often resembles an ideas competition, in which students undertake a design project developed by faculty in collaboration with external stakeholders such that the program includes real project requirements but without the pressures of actual execution.

Although hybrid projects may be viewed as a compromise, schools can use them to exert significant influence on architectural practice with significant benefits to communities. A notable example is the University of Oregon's Sustainable City Year Program, where hundreds of students enrolled in numerous courses across the university focus on projects for a single city during an entire academic year (*Sustainable City Year Program*).

Faculty who teach hybrids have greater flexibility to ensure that projects align with academic program schedules and requirements. They can adjust the focus of projects to emphasize specific learning objectives and can format assignment requirements to fully document individual student learning outcomes.

Conclusion

Educational experiences supported by Live Projects are diverse. They are also highly relevant to the education of architects and the path to professional licensure. Although there can be logistical challenges to using some types of Live Projects to fulfill accreditation requirements, Live Projects have been embraced and mainstreamed by American schools, and are an accepted approach to achieving student performance criteria defined by the NAAB. In addition, some types of Live Projects organized by schools provide experiences that fulfill requirements defined by NCARB's Intern Development Program.

The interaction between Live Projects and accreditation is a subject worthy of research. Architectural Program Reports prepared by schools and Visiting Team Reports prepared by the NAAB document how schools meet accreditation criteria. They are a valuable resource for further study that can identify best practices for the integration of Live Projects into accredited programs and strategies for improvements to accreditation processes.

References

ASCA Design-Build Award. Available online at: http://www.acsa-arch.org/programs-events/awards/design-build Accessed January 2014.

ASCA Collaborative Practice Award. Available online at: http://www.acsa-arch.org/programs-events/awards/CP Accessed January 2014.

Hayes, R.W., 2007. *The Yale Building Project*. Yale University Press.

NCARB Intern Development Program (IDP). Available online at: http://www.ncarb.org/Experience-Through-Internships.aspx Accessed January 2014.

n.a. 2009. *Conditions for Accreditation for Professional Degree Programs in Architecture*. National Architectural Accrediting Board.

NCARB Prize Program 2001–2011. Available online at: http://www.ncarb.org/Studying-Architecture/NCARB-Award/Prize-Grant/NCARB-Prize.aspx Accessed January 2014.

Rural Studio. Available online at: http://www.ruralstudio.org Accessed January 2014.

Sustainable City Year Program. Available online at: http://sci.uoregon.edu/scy Accessed January 2014.

Taliesin Student Shelters. Available online at: http://taliesin.edu/shelters/shelters1.html Accessed January 2014.

Tulane City Center. Available online at: http://www.tulanecitycenter.org/programs/university community-design-partnerships Accessed January 2014.

US Department of Energy Solar Decathlon. Available online at: http://www.solardecathlon.gov/ Accessed January 2014.

2.3

BUILDING IS ALSO A VERB

Alan Chandler

Architecture is about buildings. Is this an assumption to be challenged? At a time when writing architecture, narrative architecture, the architecture of film, of media, of programming, of 'Auto Poesis' are taking architecture into other, less physical, territories, should schools of architecture be involved with learning to build? Architecture is a discipline within academia, not an apprenticeship. The RIBA/ARB joint criteria are about ensuring professional standards, but are inevitably about standards of education, and that education is set within an academic 'higher education' framework of expectation and delivery. Do the requirements of academia impact on the professionalism of architects and, if so, what is the effect of architecture being 'academic'?

The Joint Criteria are a form of evidence of this effect as they attempt to write in a comprehensive fashion the skill-set required by the profession that needs to be evidenced at three separate stages of educational progression. Care has been taken to use terms such as 'have the ability to' in order to have students demonstrate their capacity to get it right even if they don't produce exhaustive proof, and throughout the General Criteria (for RIBA parts 1 and 2) the words 'understanding', 'understanding of', 'knowledge of', 'theoretical concepts', and 'conceptualisation' form an academic backdrop to the endeavour. These words and phrases attempt to negotiate the fact that no one can comprehensively demonstrate everything, whilst simultaneously registering that all these criteria are essential. The words themselves are intellectual and set the undertaking firmly within the world of the head, not the hand. The impact of working within and for academia is complete. Words such as 'experience', 'intuition', 'craft', and 'make' are not on this agenda, for not only do they buck the intellectualising academic trend but they, importantly, require schools of architecture to be able to deliver hand as well as head, with all the space and equipment that a making culture entails.

Freedom requires enforcement

It could be argued that the RIBA/ARB criteria do not engage with the world of making for two reasons. The first is *plurality*. This is a condition highly valued by the RIBA, and globally sets UK architecture apart from other countries with more homogeneous teaching structures. The astute wording of the criteria provides space for schools to deliver on the Criteria and Attributes without specifying how. To discuss 'building something' as a requirement would impinge on the schools' right to interpret and implement 'plurality'.

Secondly, the place of architecture schools within university structures, with the odd private exception, brings a reality to delivery that actively restricts how schools can undertake their teaching. The RIBA are clearly aware that the 'plurality' that is desirable for ideological reasons is essential for pragmatic reasons also – how many schools maintain workshops in the face of budget cuts, estates management, and health and safety requirements? Criteria that allow for diverse teaching structures are both ideologically ambitious and dirtily pragmatic.

While careful use of academic and intellectual wording allows for schools to, in principle, balance the hand and the head, the lack of requirement to do so makes the 'academicisation' of architectural education that much easier, cheaper, and more inevitable. The presentation of knowledge and the ability to evidence 'understanding' without building is encapsulated in Graduate Attribute GA2.2 – 'have the ability to evaluate and apply a comprehensive range of visual, oral and written media to test, analyse, critically appraise and explain design proposals' (RIBA 2011). Contrary to appearances, this is not a determined critique of the criteria. Instead, it is within the context of a discussion of 'Live Projects' that the scarcity of 'building as learning' processes in schools of architecture becomes starkly apparent.

The effect of 'vagueness'

The criteria describe a design process through prescribing a series of pinch-points, requirements of awareness of that process, but, crucially, leaving open the origin and purpose of the work and where and with whom the project engages. These key omissions enable 'plurality', but vagueness at these points in the design process allows education to become the inverse of practice, where precision in understanding the detail of the needs of others is paramount, and sets in motion the potential for the design process itself to achieve complete self-referentiality. '[B]etter results were obtained when the problematics of site and user were omitted' was a comment by a respected academic in conversation with the author that seemed to sum up the situation.

What is the effect of the vagueness allowable by the Joint Criteria?

A former tutor of mine asserted at a recent conference on 'Writing Architecture' that text is effectively an un-built work of architecture, and that un-built works of architecture can be as powerful as the built – additionally, they were easier for people to 'understand' than the realised building. The vagueness within the criteria concerning the purpose and meaning of an architectural project allows for an academic position that redefines architectural legibility as more likely in text than in building.

The term 'understood' needs clarification at this point, before we lose buildings altogether. By 'understanding' in the academic sense do we mean that the correct interpretation is made? Do we, as architects, require that the correct meaning – the meaning we assign as originators – is what needs to be comprehended? What happens if the wrong meaning is interpreted? Are we, as architects, running the risk of being 'misunderstood'? Architecture is complex. In reference to the founder of cybernetics Stafford Beer's definition, its practice could be said to contain too much 'requisite variety' that requires attenuation to bring it to a manageable state. As Beer himself explained in *Designing Freedom* (Beer 1974),[1] key to this attenuation is where we limit variety – before we make decisions, or as part of making decisions. Clearly, in our example the act of writing has complexity just as building does, but the core difference is in the limitation of complexity to intellectual interpretation. A building requires both intellectual and phenomenological interpretation, as well as involving issues of function, performance, and lifecycle, and it operates contextually in a way that ideas simply cannot. The architect cannot hope to control so many factors when building, so does 'building' (as a verb) mean an inevitable loss of control?

The life of a building (noun) touches the lives of those who interact with it, lives too numerous to record, with interpretations of that building too personal or too ephemeral to manage. However, a building starts its life controlled, a product of variety attenuation (planning policy, property prices, speculation, and legislation) and of management (safety, budget, team, ego, and information); yet, ironically, a building ultimately achieves complete vagueness in terms of how it is understood, used, adapted, and absorbed into 'place'. Subsequently, building (verb) born of control allows the building (noun) to ultimately escape to the vague through a life of use and abuse.

The birth of a student architecture project defined in the Joint Criteria could be text, film, building design, or Voronoi diagram, and is the inverse of a building: it begins within criteria that allow for vagueness, a defined set of control devices ensure that it attains, more or less convincingly, the control points, and a determined, compliant 'understood' outcome is achieved. We can simulate the vagueness of a real building at the end of the portfolio, but it is illusory because the processing of variety is contrived. A surrealist game of 'exquisite corpse' is a product not of the subconscious, but of the surrealists around the table sharing a pen. So, if academic architecture is an inverted 'representation' of building, how can this be addressed?

Is a 'Live Project' what is required?

If we are to go beyond the academic teaching environment because the separation between head and hand is age-old and discredited, firstly we need to articulate the process by which we can do this – so do we just 'build'?

Simply building a project one designs within the academy accomplishes the manual dexterity and material evaluation required of stable construction, we hope. The understanding of the technical limitations of materials and their manipulation delivers invaluable insights into performance, durability, effective design detailing, and judgement which are core to constructing places for people. However, the vagueness at the inception of the design project establishes the starting point for the building task that requires so much self-definition that working out a convincing set of criteria, such that a properly resolved built piece can result, is highly unlikely within an academic calendar.

If we adopt another architect's design to short-circuit the student's intellectual prevarication we can construct a previous example – say, build a 1:5 of the Farnsworth House? Or we could set new and unchallenged criteria that initiate a built study. But, inevitably, these tasks cannot provide genuine determinants that really challenge developmental and constructional processes. Construction with materials at full scale is a valuable introduction to the stuff that architects refer to and specify in a building's realisation, but, really, what is the value of getting covered in cement for a week when you supposedly have BIM (Building Information Modelling)? How or indeed why go through the charade of spending a month making a scarf joint that a decent carpenter could execute in half an hour? We could claim with justification that simply building things has an experiential value, but only up to a point; it is labour in lieu of, not as well as, critical thinking.

If a 'Live Project' is required, what is required of a Live Project?

Live Projects are live because they are about building, yes? Not necessarily. Strictly speaking, if we accept vagueness as inevitable then 'Live' may simply mean 'engaging with external agencies outside the academy'. This in itself acknowledges the benefits of dispelling vagueness in education by looking beyond the academy at the start of the design process, but the 'feasibility study', live in the sense of personal engagement with a client, does not complete the cycle of architectural design, and we are not yet approaching the specific value of learning architecture by building. 'The drawing' as an output remains untested by events, either during or after construction. A desktop study may precisely define ideas, but the accuracy of those ideas – their ability to be 'right' – will never be known. Precision and accuracy are different, and need to be brought together.

In truth, the reality of building can be experienced only by building reality. Does this imply that a 'Live Project' is only the making of a building? No – 'Live Projects' are more nuanced than this. A fully 'live' version of a project requires both the material resolution of a situation and a critical reflection on the outcome such that future professional advantage can be gained, establishing a real context for material invention. One is actually collapsing the RIBA work-stage structure and connecting strategic understanding directly with detail design and post-occupancy evaluation, all within a matters of days/weeks/months rather than years.

FIGURE 2.3.1 The international NGO Article 25 are engaged with an informal settlement in Port Harcourt, on the banks of the Niger Delta in Africa. Part of this support is the construction of a community radio station on a ground consisting of half a metre of compacted refuse on water and mud.

If the 'Live Project' educator/practitioner takes the RIBA at face value, the integration of the full gamut of work-stages within the student's experience has to be achieved unequivocally. Simply bringing students into touch with clients to 'design' is not enough to justify the use of the epithet 'Live'. Our education has to engage with the end game of architecture – people and built space – in order to contextualise the design process and allow the consequences of judgement to be understood or anticipated. Producing only speculation without dealing with its consequences leaves a vast gap in student experience and fails to deliver the outcomes required by the validating criteria.

The point of handover is the point of the project

The direct engagement of students with a building (noun) requires the direct engagement with building (verb). The sidestepping of this logic because of the structural limitations of delivering architectural education within an academic context can only continue for so long, but the 'School of Building' that nurtures critical invention as well as mere competence of execution or esoteric fantasy is still some way off.

Meanwhile, whether building real places or inventing the means by which others can build their own, all students of architecture should be given the opportunity to understand the consequences of their education while they are still learning:

FIGURE 2.3.2 Technical needs and requirements are critically incorporated into extreme 'low-tech' – a 1:1 prototype utilised compacted refuse rammed into adapted plastic buckets to create simple waffle slabs to save on cement and achieve a 32 per cent concrete saving.

Overall, understanding the real needs of the people in Nigeria, and the necessity to adapt the construction of the foundations on a 1:1 scale, were proved to be the greatest challenges. These two points in the project were the most important, as they brought out the practical problems that men and women on the Delta might have to deal with. If the project ended with the calculations and analysis of smaller models, such obstacles would have passed unseen, failing if actually built on site.

(Beer 1974)

Vagueness, like education, 'constrains variety, because although it may open new vistas, it leads us to reduce the alternatives that we are prepared to entertain ...' (Beer 1974).

Note

1 According to Jackson (2000), 'Beer was the first to apply cybernetics to management, defining cybernetics as the science of effective organization.'

References

Beer, S. (1974). *Designing Freedom*. Wiley.
Jackson, M. C. (2000). *Systems Approaches to Management*. Kluwer Academic.

RIBA. (2011). 'RIBA Procedures for Validation and Validation Criteria'. RIBA Education Department. Available online at: http://www.architecture.com/Files/RIBAProfessional Services/Education/Validation/ValidationProcedures2011.pdf Accessed January 2014.

Taylor, H., Grimaldi, S., Fineberg, L., Wood, L., Phipps, J., Nokano, Y., and Kalawashoti, M. (2012). Port Harcourt, Technical Report, UEL, unpublished.

2.4

LIVE PROJECTS AT MID-CENTURY: A PRE-HISTORY

Nils Gore

In 1954, in an AIA report entitled "The Architect at Mid-century: Evolution and Achievement," Ralph Walker presciently noted:

> In some parts of the world architects are already fearful that *industrialization* in building will affect them adversely; ... that the builder and the manufacturer will take over the design of the stereotype buildings. ... There is, however, a great need for the master-designer fully conversant with construction require-ments who can take leadership not only in production of architectural and engineering design but also in guiding the actual building in the field . . . . These circumstances and factors have important implications for the education of an architect.
>
> *(Bannister 1954: xiv)*

And, later in the same book:

> For some architects and educators, the gap between school and practice seems too wide to bridge. Professor Gropius, for example, wrote in 1950: "Should architectural education then be separated from its *present academic framework*? Many architects would agree with a decisive turn towards greater emphasis on practical experience. I, personally, have grave doubts as to whether the present *bookish climate of universities* can offer at all a healthy breeding ground for architects. ... [T]he greatest strength of American technical education lies in its development of ingenious demonstration apparatus and the provision of *teaching laboratories* in which students are led by carefully controlled projects to intimate knowledge of materials and their manipulation."
>
> *(ibid.: 153; emphasis mine)*

Some 40 years later, a handful of universities in the US (Yale, Auburn, University of Kansas) started implementing significant design/build studios. Today, it is reported that 100 out of 123 schools of architecture in the US have some kind of design/build program (Gjertson 2011).

Why would something so clear to leaders such as Gropius and Walker take so long to be institutionalized in schools of architecture? And why is there still doubt among architectural educators about it?

Institutional inertia

Institutional inertia is the tendency for organizations to solidify their way of being in the world (Hannan and Freeman 1984; Kingston and Caballero 2009). In the early twentieth century, when our profession was securing its foothold in the larger culture of building, the AIA asserted that "he who bears the title of architect has the knowledge and ability needed for the proper invention, illustration, and supervision of all building operations which he may undertake. Such qualifications alone justify the assumption of the title of architect" ("Circular of Advice Relative to Principles of Practice and the Canons of Ethics" (AIA Document 163) cited in King 1922: 311). Additionally, "It is unprofessional for an architect − 1. To engage directly or indirectly in any of the building or decorative trades." Because builders have a vested interest in the cost, process, and outcome of a construction project, they apparently lack the level of detachment required for professional imprimatur: "An architect's honesty of purpose must be above suspicion; he renders professional services to his client and acts as his client's agent and adviser. His advice to his client must be sound and unprejudiced, as he is charged with the exercise of impartial judgment in interpreting contract documents" (AIA Document J-330 1964).

Oddly, according to the same standards of practice, the architect is responsible for "invention, illustration, and supervision of all building operations." One might fairly ask, how should the aspiring architect gain knowledge of construction? In that era construction generally adhered to traditional standards; workmen tended to follow best practices and exhibited pride in their work (Davis 1999). Buildings were simpler, material palettes were limited, and mechanical/electrical systems were few (Kieran and Timberlake 2004). Young architects' first assignments were to "trace designs done by more experienced people in the office," thus learning, by rote, construction details (Davis 1999: 64). By the time architects ascended to responsibility, they likely had gained the requisite knowledge. Organizationally, owners, architects, and contractors were primarily small, independent entities, operating cooperatively on local projects (ibid.: 66; Garber 2009). Relative to the canons of ethics of the time, the system worked.

A university education and professional internships were both paths into the profession. Unlike the practical training of interns, students completing the university path received a broader liberal base of learning intended to "cultivat[e] intellectual and ethical judgment, helping students comprehend and negotiate their relationship to the larger world, and preparing graduates for lives of civic responsibility and leadership" (Schneider 2004). In the face of an increasingly complex world following the Second World War, university-based professional education became the norm throughout the US and Western Europe (Boyer and Mitgang 1996).

Bannister's disparagement of the "bookish climate of universities" is a common one, rooted in the perception of colleges as cloistered communities of learned scholars surrounded by books in arcane languages and engaged in discussion of little practical use (Hofstadter 2012). At the same time, vocational education was perceived as "the kind of education whose chief aim is to promote the capacity to earn a living or, expressed in more social terms, the capacity to do one's share of the productive work of the world. ... Vocational education has ... its own pedagogy; and its methods may even be in opposition to those of liberal education" (Snedden 1910: 4–6). Perkin characterizes the university as "transformed from a seminary for priests and a finishing school for gentlemen into a professional school for every expert occupation" (Perkin 2002: 5).

It's hard to know exactly when the system stopped working well, but the end of World War II, the rise of technocratic society, and a burgeoning middle class have something to do with it (Bledstein 1978). In the US, the GI bill expanded educational opportunities to a class of people who wouldn't have had access prior to the war, and postwar prosperity fueled new building projects beyond the institutions and wealthy individuals accustomed to hiring architects. The rise of the corporate developer client, with more mercenary (as opposed to symbolic) business objectives, and the rise of a more professionalized and organized construction sector undoubtedly played a role (Finkel 1997). More technically complex building programs, systems, and assemblies further destabilized the practice of architecture. Hence Bannister's discomfort in the mid-1950s with the perceived shortcomings of architectural education, which now seemed inadequate to confront the exertions of postwar capitalism.

In 1970 the federal government in the US struck a significant blow to the professions when it ruled that the Sherman Antitrust act should be applied to the professions' use of minimum fee schedules, declaring them "a means of price fixing" by commercial – as opposed to professional – entities and therefore illegal (Walzer 1972: 439). This ruling forced modifications to the AIA's Canon of Ethics, opening the door to architect selection by fee rather than qualification. In 1978 the ethical stricture against architects engaging in construction was eliminated by a vote of the AIA membership and design/build project delivery became a legitimate avenue of practice (Block 1984: 8). Raging inflation in the 1970s spurred "fast-track" construction management services by actors in the construction industry, who assumed an advisory role to building owners and displaced architects from the sole advisory position. In each instance, the clarity of the architect's societal role diminished and the architect's self-conception as a detached, selfless professional became less narrowly defined.

Looked at objectively (which is nigh impossible in the midst of rapid change), it should have been clear that it was a new world. But most architects just felt the increase in pressure and tried to behave as they always had. Legal agreements had their own inertia. Office policies and procedures didn't change overnight. Builders, banks, and realtors didn't radically alter their self-conceptions. The culture of building is vast and slow to change: an ocean liner does not turn on a dime.

In hindsight, it seems obvious that architecture school pedagogies would need revision. But institutional inertia is strong in the self-conception of both the architect and the universities. It's no wonder that it took 40 years to get around to having architecture students actually build something in the studio, then another 20 for it really to catch on in a majority of schools. Universities, despite the trumpeting of liberal ideas and ideals, are some of the most conservative institutions, perhaps because faculties are self-governed. In the absence of external forces requiring change in curricula and policies, they prefer to maintain the status quo than to engage in the hard work of persuading reluctant colleagues to respond to exigencies in the external world. Most professors truly believe in the value of the subject matter they teach; it is personally costly to invent new coursework (Lipset 1982: 154). Unless space and equipment can be procured with research or endowment dollars, it is hard to justify to faculty and upper administration why scarce resources should be spent on tools and construction labs when the value to the profession is not patently clear. After all, similar institutional inertias are at work in the profession: the vast majority of architects still engage in a strictly traditional approach to their work. They design buildings, observe their construction in a detached way, and administer the contract for construction. Neither entity – schools nor profession – wishes to take on any liability not required. It took a few courageous individual faculty – and a few bold university administrators – to make the initial forays into substantial student design/build projects. As those early projects were disseminated in the popular professional press and the scholarly academic press they gained attention, and other faculty and schools joined in. Their adoption over time, as legitimate pedagogical practices, climbed exponentially.

Since the turn of the twenty-first century pressures are coming at the architecture profession and its educational partners from numerous directions. Global climate change is an existential threat; catastrophic financial collapse has forced change on the culture of building; university funding streams have been curtailed; educational models and delivery methods have been reinvented; new construction business strategies have been developed. The technologies of representation change with each passing year, and, with them, relationships to fabricators, manufacturers, and consultants. Building systems and assemblies have become more sophisticated (and unknown). Instant communication with international partners enables new ways of being in the world.

Yet we still have at most five years to train productive professional citizens. There is abundant innovation in higher education right now. Lumping them together under the heading of "engaged learning," we find flipped and hybrid interactive classroom environments (as opposed to the passive, talking-head lecture), online delivery, study abroad, public interest design, and service learning. Design Thinking has emerged outside of traditional design education – particularly business. In that context, design/build projects in architecture school, rather than being erroneously thought of as "vocational" training in the building crafts, should be considered an active, engaged learning strategy to promote learning and brain development in ways that couldn't be done in the traditional design studio. We are past the point of having to justify these projects' existence. We need to evolve them into something even better.

References

AIA Document J-330 (1964). "The Standards of Professional Practice." *Architect's Handbook of Professional Practice.* American Institute of Architects.

Bannister, Turpin C. (ed.) (1954). *The Architect at Mid-Century: Evolution and Achievement. Volume 1 of Report of the Commission for the Survey of Education and Registration of the American Institute of Architects.* Reinhold.

Bledstein, Burton J. (1978). *The Culture of Professionalism: The Middle Class and the Development of Higher Education in America.* W. W. Norton.

Block, Hal G. (1984). "As the Walls Came Tumbling Down: Architects' Expanded Liability under Design–Build/Construction Contracting." *John Marshall Law Review,* 17: 1–48.

Boyer, Ernest L. and Mitgang, Lee D. (1996). *Building Community: A New Future for Architecture Education and Practice Special Report.* Carnegie Foundation for the Advancement of Teaching.

Davis, Howard (1999). *The Culture of Building.* Oxford University Press.

Finkel, Gerald (1997). *The Economics of the Construction Industry.* M. E. Sharpe.

Garber, Richard (2009). "Alberti's Paradigm." *Architectural Design,* 79(2): doi:10.1002/ad.859.

Gjertson, W. Geoff (2011). "House Divided: Challenges to Design/Build from Within." In *Proceedings of the Association of Collegiate Schools of Architecture (ACSA) 2011 Fall Conference.* ACSA.

Hannan, Michael T. and Freeman, John (1984). "Structural Inertia and Organizational Change." *American Sociological Review,* 49(2): 149–164.

Hofstadter, Richard (2012). *Anti-Intellectualism in American Life.* Illustrated edn. Random House.

Kieran, Stephen and Timberlake, James (2004). *Refabricating Architecture.* McGraw-Hill.

King, Clyde Langdon (1922). "The Ethics of the Professions and of Business." *Annals of the American Academy of Political and Social Science,* 101.

Kingston, Christopher and Caballero, Gonzalo (2009). "Comparing Theories of Institutional Change." *Journal of Institutional Economics,* 5(2): 151–180.

Lipset, Seymour Martin (1982). "The Academic Mind at the Top: The Political Behavior and Values of Faculty Elites." *Public Opinion Quarterly,* 46(2): 143–168.

Perkin, Harold (2002). *The Third Revolution: Professional Elites in the Modern World.* Routledge.

Schneider, Carol Geary (2004). "Practicing Liberal Education: Formative Themes in the Reinvention of Liberal Learning." *Liberal Education,* Spring issue: 6–11.

Snedden, David (1910). *The Problem of Vocational Education.* Houghton Mifflin Company.

Walzer, Roy S. (1972). "Minimum Fee Schedules as Price Fixing: A Per Se Violation of the Sherman Act." *American University Law Review,* 22: 439–454.

PART III

From education into practice

3.1

TEAMBUILD

New formats for delivery of learning in construction

Alex MacLaren

Introduction

The Teambuild Competition provides a tested format that delivers client-centred inter-professional learning based on projects of social and technical design complexity. The brief for this annual competition is a 'Live Project' with real data and challenges, and the resulting presentations are judged by active construction professionals and clients.

The education of architects could become less insular, more engaging, more ambiguous. Critique of the architect's role is a threshold concept given too small a part in many curricula. Teambuild posits an inclusive horizontal approach to teaching, learning, and research, alongside professional engagement. Recent graduates act as architectural consultant in an interdisciplinary team and are encouraged to critique their role.

This case study references data and my own experience gathered over seven years' involvement in Teambuild. Reference is also made to pedagogic research. I propose the benefit of this format to industry, academia, and the student, including reference to the RIBA/ARB criteria.

Context

The professional and educational contexts of architecture are undergoing rapid change. In UK practice, the industry is driven by the Government Construction Strategy towards ever more collaborative, inter-professional work (Cabinet Office 2011) with the aim of improving efficiency by a staggering 15 per cent in ten years. Simultaneously, the traditional role of the 'professional' is questioned by an increasingly commercialised global society and governmental policies empowering the public voice, exemplified in new planning policy that hands more power to local communities (National Planning Policy Framework 2012).

In UK education, moreover, we face the introduction of fees of £9,000 pa for prospective students, as the European Commission consults on raising the minimum requirement for architectural education from four to five years of full-time study (European Commission 2011). Graduates can expect starting salaries 25 per cent lower than those of other professions covered by that directive (Prospects: www.prospects.ac.uk). Current statistics from the RIBA (RIBA 2011) indicate that only 30 per cent of the students commencing a Part 1 degree are likely to qualify as an architect in the UK.

Current practices in architectural education

'Traditional' forms of architectural education have come under much criticism (Till 2009; Parnell 2003; Latham 1994) for poorly serving the student and the profession. At the core of these criticisms lies the unhelpful disjunction of education from practice, and of students from clients, users, and the construction team. 'Live Projects', pioneered by several UK schools of architecture (e.g. Sheffield, Oxford Brookes, LMU), seek to bridge this gulf and reconnect the student to the public and the profession. These projects tend to sit alongside traditional studio design projects in the curriculum. Chiles and Till argue in their case study for CEBE (Chiles and Till 2004) that the main limits to Live Projects are 'money, health and safety, and time'. A further constraint is scale and design sophistication: a term-long Live Project is unlikely to be of sufficient size or complexity to satisfy the design requirements of the RIBA criteria at Part 2 level. Teambuild models a format which could remedy these needs.

The Teambuild UK competition

'Teambuild UK' has been run in various guises for 20 years, working with young practitioners in the construction industry aged under 30. Architects form the second-largest professional group participating: 15.67 per cent over the past 17 years. Prospective entrants can register as individuals or as teams; teams must be multidisciplinary and are often entered by large construction consultancies or 'real' project teams.

The annual competition is based on an actual large-scale development underway in the UK. In 2011 this was Bicester Eco-Town; in 2012 Teambuild was partnered with the King's Cross site north of the new Central Saint Martin's college. During a weekend in November, finalist teams speed through concept, bid, appointment, design, tender, procurement, construction, and inhabitation in 48 hours via a pre-scripted set of hypothetical narratives designed to mimic the often unpredictable progress of an actual project. Entrants have time prior to the event to prepare site information, but no prior knowledge of subsequent changes to brief or scenario over the weekend. At each stage the narrative opens a question(s) relating to the project, to be answered usually within 1.5–2 hours. Questions deal with any aspect of a project, from high-level risk/opportunity analyses to strategic design to client

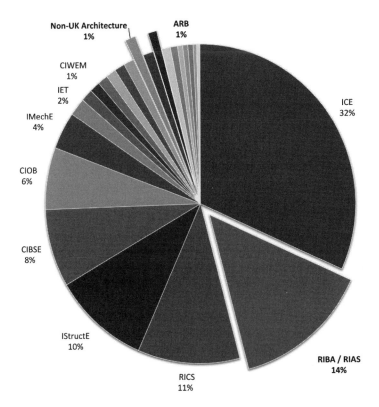

FIGURE 3.1.1 Institutions represented at Teambuild 1999–2011.

inhabitation. No team will be able to answer all the questions from its knowledge base; participants must take on other roles at each stage to support the team endeavour; different team members must lead when their specialisation is brought to the fore.

The 'real' site team and stakeholders send judge(s) to form a cross-industry panel. Site information is real and detailed; the technical, spatial, and social scenarios are intractable and complex. Technical scenarios are purely a means to require teamwork and collaborative innovation; teams are marked on their communication, teamwork, and presentation. Teambuild's complex technical scenario and design brief also tests participants' 'soft' skills: management, communication, listening, presenting.

The principal aim of Teambuild is to improve competitors' knowledge of their professional context, and specifically to improve their 'soft' skills: listening and communicating effectively. Prizes are awarded for achievement in collaboration and communication, and feedback confirms that this is where competitors feel they most improve throughout the experience.

The Chair of the Trustees and founder of the competition, Richard Rooley, discovered in the course of his presidency of ASHRAE (American Society of Heating,

FIGURE 3.1.2 A team presents their work to judges at the 'Detailed Design' stage.

FIGURE 3.1.3 Preparing a presentation to the client and local Building Control officer on site setup and construction strategy.

Refrigerating and Air Conditioning Engineers) that active members employed in consulting firms spent only 20 per cent of their working week on technical material, and the rest managing and communicating with colleagues and clients (Rooley 2007). It is noted that the 2011 revision of the RIBA/ARB Criteria (RIBA/ARB 2010) removes any mention of 'communication' from the 44 General Criteria at Parts 1 and 2. Teambuild addresses this overlooked but immensely important area.

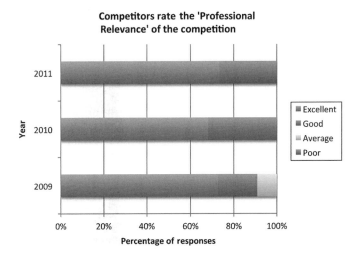

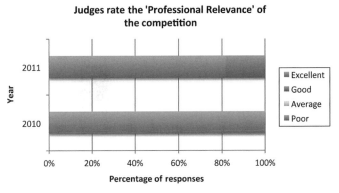

FIGURE 3.1.4 Competitors and judges rate the 'Professional Relevance' of the competition.

Analysis of the competition

Pedagogic evaluation

Many students do not realise that the 'role of the architect' is a complex threshold concept (Cousin 2006). Teambuild offers a context in which young professionals must explore this role personally and may critique their efforts. Their interpretation of the role is unrestricted. The format encourages recursive learning and experimentation.

First-time competitors at Teambuild are new to this kind of trans-disciplinary, inter-reliant team, and are faced immediately with a complex brief and tangible outcomes required within an extremely short timeframe. Immediate communication challenges are posed, as individuals from different professional backgrounds often interpret the brief and deliverables differently. Ambiguity can lead to anxiety, as each team member must work hard to communicate her or his understanding to other members and together arrive quickly at a plan of action. Empathy is established quickly. Individuals acquire a new way of looking at a problem: they realise their role in relation to others, and what they can offer to this team. The situation is similar to that studied by Harriss and Cassels in their project involving architecture and MBA students in 2010 (Harriss and Cassells 2010). It further develops competitors' critical analysis and 'understanding of the systems in which they [will] operate' (Berryman and Bailey 1992), skills that Berryman and Bailey argue are essential within modern education in order for graduates to prosper in the workplace. In this way the pedagogic model of Teambuild can be likened to the 'cognitive apprenticeships' suggested in that text.

Feedback sessions form an integral part of the programme. Feedback is structured in order to inform teams' subsequent work, enabling an effective experiential learning cycle. Competitors and judges alike find the sessions useful in gauging the level of assessment and critique and improving team communication. The mix of disciplines and the divorce of 'brief-writer' and 'tutor/judge' encourages open discussion, enabling further learning benefits (Parnell 2001).

Assessment procedures

Teambuild has not been run in or by a higher education institution to date. Finalists achieve four days' equivalent CPD and many competitors take part in preparation for their various Chartership/RIBA Part 3 exams, but it is not recognised as part of a formal qualification. Consequently the competition is not bound by regulatory assessment criteria or process requirements, and this has allowed the organisers to explore methods of assessment. Internal reviews have found that minimising constraints in production, deliverables, and assessment and providing contingency within the competition framework have successfully produced an effective learning environment. In short, learning is improved by not restricting the engagement of competitors with their 'clients' and by relinquishing control over the practical outcome.

The various judges rotate at each stage so that they encounter each team an equal number of times. In this way teams receive critique and opinion from varied standpoints and are evaluated from different perspectives. These evaluations can be contradictory. This itself is a valuable learning experience (Morrow *et al.* 2001).

The separation of 'brief-writer' from 'principal assessor' is extraordinarily valuable in encouraging exploration and innovation. Competitors cannot takes cues from tutors to find a perceived 'correct answer'. Further disjunction is afforded by the briefs' demand for technical application and prowess, although this part of the submission will not be assessed. This does not have the impact of reducing experiment and invention; individuals wish to demonstrate their flair to both peers and judges without fear of failure. Technical achievement is discussed and critiqued, but not graded, and this opportunity to 'show and tell' in a competitive environment free from direct assessment proves peculiarly liberating for designers.

Relation to ARB/RIBA criteria

The current ARB/RIBA criteria (RIBA/ARB 2010) comprise 44 General Criteria shared between Parts 1 and 2, qualified at different levels of achievement by 10 or 11 'Graduate Attributes' for each level. These criteria are mapped directly over the 11 points of the European Parliament Qualifications Directive 2005.

The criteria reflect the progressive move towards early-stage interdisciplinary teamworking in the industry and the increased role of the client. Four of the criteria cite relationships with 'co-professionals' and five refer to the needs of 'building users'. 'Understanding ... the role of the architect in society ... [and] within the design team and construction industry' forms a core part of GC6, a requirement at both Parts 1 and 2. The experience of working within a multi-disciplinary team for real clients, as offered by Teambuild, gives participants direct experience on which to base this understanding and the confidence to question their role in a known context.

The pre-2011 criteria for architectural education divided neatly into five sectors. Curricula often considered these categories independently and educated in 'silos' accordingly. The current criteria cannot be sectioned in this way, as shown below. This hybrid framework now requires a synthesis of historically disjointed parts of the curriculum, a new looser, horizontal, and inclusive pedagogy similar to that achieved by the Teambuild competition.

The differing levels of achievement laid over shared criteria provide a challenge to the educator: how to teach the same content while assessing at different levels of success. Teambuild offers an identical, extremely complex brief and site information to teams of young professionals aged from 19 to 29. The teams' achievements vary but their learning is equally valuable. Past competitors are invited to return and compete again if they have not won; several do, and feedback confirms that they learn more and differently the second time. This also supports the theory that threshold concepts benefit from recursive learning (Cousin 2006).

Relationships to industry

Teambuild introduces young graduates to intensive working with their industry peers at an earlier stage than usually demanded in practice. The competition also brings competitors into contact with senior industry figures and employers serving as judges. Contact with industry is especially valuable for graduates' confidence, and 'early contact with employers' is specifically noted as a 'key issue' in the drive to encourage greater diversity in the profession (CABE 2005).

Contact with industry also opens up alternative sources for expertise and funding. Teambuild has found that sponsorship opportunities are attractive to a wide range of professional institutions, consultancies, manufacturers, and suppliers, in addition to training and educational trusts. Sponsorship packages require sponsors to provide experienced judges for the competition weekend, as well as cash funding. Both parties view this as a mutually beneficial relationship. The competition is currently sponsored by the ICE, CIOB, CIBSE, the IStructE Educational Trust,

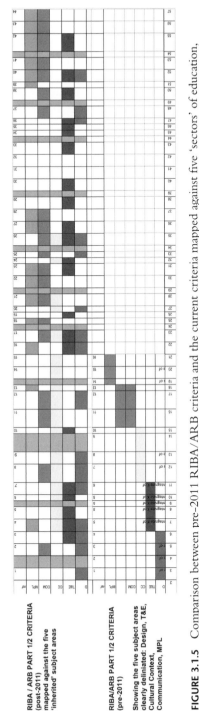

FIGURE 3.1.5 Comparison between pre-2011 RIBA/ARB criteria and the current criteria mapped against five 'sectors' of education, showing the new hybrid nature of the requirements.

Speedyhire Ltd, and Saint-Gobain Ltd, and supported by the RIBA, RICS, SCL, and the A G Manly Trust. These sponsors not only demonstrate their foresight in investing in training but also offer us expertise. They engage the interest of motivated graduates in the future of our industry.

Conclusion

As a practitioner I am apprehensive about yet encouraged by the potential of the architectural profession in the UK as we explore the impact of new forms of procurement and construction. As a tutor I am concerned about how best to equip students to lead the profession in this new context and how to deliver educational value worthy of the now extraordinary levels of both time and financial commitment required. As a trustee of Teambuild I see a way to improve delivery in both of these preoccupations.

I have discussed elements of the training competition that may be applied to architectural curricula to improve learning in several themes: teamworking in situations of ambiguity; realisation of threshold concepts of the role of the architect; professional communication; design collaboration; a means of assessment in 'Live Project' environments; self-awareness in a professional context. Key lessons to consider in seeking to translate benefits into emerging academic curricula might be engagement with industry; hybrid cross-disciplinary deliverables; client engagement or role-playing; and, finally, divorcing brief-setting from critique.

References

Berryman, S.E. and Bailey, T. (1992). *The Double Helix of Education and the Economy*. Institute of Education and the Economy.

CABE (Commission for Architecture and the Built Environment) (2005). *Minority Ethnic Representation in the Built Environment Professions*. Centre for Ethnic Minority Studies, Royal Holloway, University of London.

Cabinet Office (2011). *Government Construction Strategy*. London.

Chiles, P. and Till, J. (2004). 'Live Projects: An Inspirational Model. The Student Perspective'. CEBE case study. Available online at: http://cebe.cf.ac.uk/learning/casestudies/case_pdf/PrueChiles.pdf Accessed January 2014.

Cousin, G. (2006). 'An Introduction to Threshold Concepts'. *Planet*, 17. Available online at: http://www.gees.ac.uk/planet/p17/gc.pdf Accessed January 2014.

European Commission (2011). Green Paper: 'Modernising the Professional Qualifications Directive', Article 46, Options 1 and 2. Brussels.

Harriss, H. and Cassells, E. (2010). 'Learning from Ambiguity within an Interdisciplinary Teaching and Learning Context.' Oxford Brookes Learning and Teaching Conference.

Latham, Sir M. (1994). 'Constructing the Team'. *Joint Review of Procurement and Contractual Arrangements in the United Kingdom Construction Industry*. Final Report HMSO.

Morrow, R., Parnell, R. and Torrington, J. (2001). 'Reality versus Creativity?' Architectural Education Exchange. Available online at: http://cebe.cf.ac.uk/transactions/pdf/RuthMorrow.pdf Accessed January 2014.

National Planning Policy Framework (2012). https://www.gov.uk/government/publications/national-planning-policy-framework-2 Accessed January 2014.

Parnell, R. (2001). 'It's Good to Talk: Managing Disjunction through Peer Discussion'. Architectural Education Exchange. Available online at: http://cebe.cf.ac.uk/ee/sessions/ http://cebe.cf.ac.uk/aee/pdfs/parnellr.pdf Accessed January 2014.

Parnell, R. (2003) 'Knowledge Skills and Arrogance: Educating for Collaborative Practice'. EAAE Prize 2001–2002. Available online at: http://www.academia.edu/508750/Knowledge_Skills_and_Arrogance_Educating_for_Collaborative_ Practice Accessed January 2014.

Prospects, the UK's official graduate careers website. Available online at: www.prospects.ac.uk Accessed January 2014.

RIBA (2011). 'Education Statistics 2010–2011'. RIBA Centre for Architectural Education.

RIBA/ARB (2010). 'Criteria for Validation 2011'. RIBA Publications.

Rooley, R.H. (2007). 'Worst Practice Lessons for Energy Efficiency'. ASHRAE conference paper.

Till, J. (2009) *Architecture Depends*. Routledge.

3.2

THE GRAD PROGRAMME

Live Project peer enablement

Sebastian Messer

Introduction

The Northern Architecture Graduate Retention and Development (GRAD) programme[1] is a collaboration between built environment graduates seeking relevant experience and employment, community-based organisations, architectural practices, and schools of architecture in the region. It commenced in January 2010 in response to the economic situation affecting employment opportunities for graduates of architecture and other built environment disciplines in the region. Its participants (known as GRADs) identify problems with design-based solutions and how those projects may lead to funded work – either for the graduates or for local practices.

The aims of the GRAD programme are to:

- improve the participants' portfolios and CVs and aid their prospects for full-time employment;
- benefit the participants directly by developing their knowledge, confidence, and skills and providing a forum for peer support and assistance;
- benefit the region by retaining talent in the North East and identifying problems that may have a design-based solution; and
- develop opportunities potentially leading to funded work, either for the programme's participants or for local practitioners.

The aims are encapsulated by the 'Three Ps':

Produce | Present | Potential

The right projects

The founding members of the GRAD programme agreed upon the criteria by which we would select projects so that they would:

- not exploit the participants' voluntary labour,
- not undercut or take work away from other professionals or consultants,
- provide learning opportunities for the participants,
- be relevant, interesting, and challenging, and
- produce tangible results.

The first cohort

The first cohort had graduated from UK architecture degree courses and had been seeking Part I architectural assistant positions for around six months when the GRAD programme commenced. They chose the name archiGRAD to identify their 'practice'. To date, one other 'franchise' has been founded, with MADE*, in August 2012.

MADEgrads

In August 2012, we were invited to MADE*, the Architecture Centre for the West Midlands, to present the GRAD programme. During the subsequent discussion, four graduates from Birmingham City University and one graduate from Sheffield University spontaneously formed MADEgrads. In October 2012, they moved out of MADE's office into space provided by Bryan Priest Newman. By the summer of 2013, there had been 27 participants, with current GRADs undertaking a feasibility study for a bandstand in Solihull and creating architectural models for the 'Birmingham Made Me' expo.

Comparable models in the UK

While we knew of 'Project Offices' situated within schools of architecture and summer schools offering design-build experience for a fee, at the time the GRAD programme commenced there was only one comparable model in the UK.

RIBA Host Practice

The RIBA Host Practice scheme (Royal Institute of British Architects 2011, 2009) proposed that practices making redundancies should offer surplus workstations to graduates. This would not be an internship, as the Host Practice scheme requires the graduate to have already secured work or devised research to undertake during a three-month residency. The graduates benefit from facilities available in the practice, including licensed software, the experience of being in an office environment, and mentoring. Potentially, however, the graduate could become isolated, having neither a wider network of peer-support nor being fully part of the host practice.

Getting started

Initially we secured seed funding of £200 from Northumbria University and approached Newcastle University for a matching sum. Further contributions of £250 were received from each university after 18 and 36 months. In 2012, the Northern Architectural Association donated £350 to the programme.

Notionally, that equates to £15 per participant to pay for materials, printing, postage, website hosting, and digital data storage, ensuring that participation in the programme does not financially disadvantage the GRADs.

The role of local universities and practices

We decided to make the GRAD programme 'arms' length' from both Northumbria and Newcastle Universities to ensure that all graduates have equal access to it.

By July 2013 there had been 121 participants in archiGRAD, who had graduated from institutions all over the UK. Sixty per cent of the participants in archiGRAD have been offered paid graduate employment within four months of commencing. Both GRADs and their employers cite the experience in archiGRAD as the principal reason they were offered a job.

Increasingly, both local universities refer project enquiries to archiGRAD, which is promoted to third-year students in both institutions as an option for 'year-out' experience. Both also recognise the benefit of keeping alumni in the region for their retention of postgraduate students.

Local practices, with links to both architectural education and Northern Architecture, were supportive of the programme's objective. We requested that they provide contact details for archiGRAD in the rejection letters they sent to unsuccessful job applicants, widening awareness of the programme among graduates who had studied outside the North East.

archiGRAD also acts as an informal employment agency, allowing participants to promote themselves through the archiGRAD website (http://www.archiGRAD. co.uk) as a pool of architectural 'temps' for local practices requiring particular skills for short term contracts. A number of local practices also regularly approach archiGRAD before advertising new vacancies.

Supportive practices continue to be involved. In 2011 and 2012 directors from twelve North East practices joined in 'speed dating' style events to offer advice to graduating students on their CVs and portfolios. They have also hosted archiGRAD Summer Schools, providing office-based experience and mentoring to architecture students from Newcastle and Northumbria Universities in intermediate years.

archiGRAD Summer Schools

In 2012 the School of Architecture, Planning and Landscape at Newcastle University commissioned Northern Architecture to pilot a Summer School, based on the GRAD programme model. Four North East architectural practices (+£ Architecture, Faulknerbrowns, Hugh Massey Architects and xsite Architecture) plus one 'client', the Globe Gallery (with mentoring from Medical Architecture), hosted and mentored the six-week Summer Schools. Two participants were offered Part I positions following the 2012 Summer Schools. In 2013 three Summer Schools were hosted by +3 Architecture, Faulknerbrowns and xsite Architecture.

Professional recognition

Dundee, Huddersfield, Leeds Metropolitan, Newcastle, and Northumbria Universities will all recognise 20 certified hours per week on archiGRAD projects contributes up to three months of the participants' Professional Experience and Development Record (PEDR).[2]

However, the actual take-up by participants has been lower than expected, with only 10 per cent registering for PEDR. Those who have not registered cite the costs of both the online PEDR system and the universities' 'year-out' modules as the main disincentive.

The projects

At the time of writing, archiGRAD has completed 27 projects ranging in scale and type from the devising and running of community consultation and participatory events (Figure 3.2.1) through speculative design projects and design competitions, architectural, landscape, and urban analysis and design projects, and small-scale realised projects and exhibitions to a flythrough of a virtual cityscape produced for an immersive theatre production.[3]

Consultancy gap

During discussions with our 'clients' about their prior experiences, we realised that the GRAD programme was filling a 'Consultancy Gap' between a 'client' identifying a problem and the stage at which, for instance, a grant can be sought to fund further development or realisation of the project.

The GRAD programme creates 'shared-value', a concept devised in Harvard Business School (Kramer and Porter 2011). Shared-value redefines the measure of economic 'value-added' by a business to include societal benefits relative to their cost, not merely net profits, leading to increased innovation and productivity and expanding opportunities for value creation.

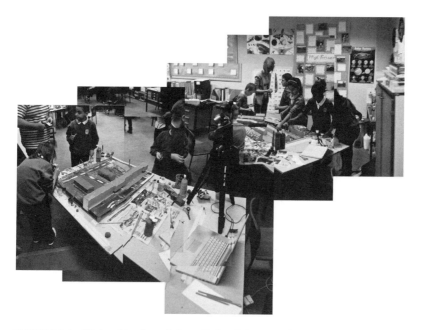

FIGURE 3.2.1 'Byker Lives' workshop, Byker Primary School.

The 'win-win-win' created thus benefits:

- The 'clients' – who are better able to articulate a brief describing their needs and ambitions to funding bodies and to professional consultants, thereby avoiding abortive work and expense. Providing conceptual design solutions can also facilitate consultation with, or encourage 'buy-in' from, the wider community.
- The GRADs themselves – who gain relevant professional experience, make contacts beyond the narrow confines of their peer group and may be employed by an architect to develop the project they helped instigate. The programme could 'hothouse' GRADs testing their own business ideas or developing an archiGRAD project into their own business.
- Architects and other consultants – for whom new projects have been created and who will be able to work with a better-informed client and a defined brief.

Baltic Education Pavilion

The Baltic Centre for Contemporary Art approached archiGRAD for ideas for a bespoke, demountable structure to replace the marquees they hired commercially for events. archiGRAD developed concept designs (Figure 3.2.2), but Baltic were not able to proceed after their Arts Council grant was reduced. Under their charitable remit, the Baltic Floor Mills Visual Arts Trust offered to assist a GRAD to apply for funding to enable the design to be developed and prototyped as a business start-up.

FIGURE 3.2.2 Visualisation of the Baltic Education Pavilion (Alex Davies).

Challenges to GRAD self-management

Recognising many GRADs are also in part-time or full-time employment, the programme allows them to commit as much time as they feel able and to stay involved for as long as they find it useful. This presents particular challenges for the management of the programme and running of the projects.

In the first twelve months there was a steep learning curve for the mentors. Optimistically, we had assumed the participants would be able to organise themselves, manage their time, and seek out and develop their own project briefs before we realised the majority had neither the skills nor the experience for this level of self-management.

Project champions

Following our realisation that the programme required management by the mentors, responsibility for the individual projects was devolved to the participants. The idea of Project Champions evolved organically as a number of Part II graduates in the second cohort were willing to take leading roles. Project Champions are self-selecting or selected by the team interested in working on a particular brief. A GRAD ought to be a Project Champion for only one project at a time, although he or she may also be contributing to a number of other projects.

The Project Champions' role is administrative. They prepare documentation, consolidating the brief and a project programme and producing a proforma 'Design Report'. They also arrange times when the project team will work together and report on progress at meetings with the mentors and with 'clients'. However, while the Project Champion becomes the main point of contact, the GRAD ethos is to encourage collaboration and teamwork.

Teamwork

Teamwork is expedient in pooling ideas, which accelerates the design process. Usually this will lead to unexpected design propositions for which the whole team feel ownership and share in the 'symbolic capital' (Rajkovics 2012) connected with success. It also creates a useful, critical distance for the mentors from the work produced by the GRADs.

The whole body of work is available for all GRADs to include in their personal portfolio, as well as demonstrating their ability to work collaboratively.

The design process

All projects follow a similar sequence of problem-setting and problem-solving.

A new brief is 'pitched' to the cohort at the mentoring meeting and a Project Champion nominated. An initial phase of data collection is undertaken, including site visit, desktop study, and collecting of precedent images for inspiration.

The subsequent discussion often may also include a critique of the language of the brief. For instance, 'What is a "creative quarter"?' 'Are there three other "quarters" and if so, what are they?' and so on. This can reveal both the GRADs' and the 'client's' preconceptions (Figure 3.2.3). Making these preconceptions explicit and

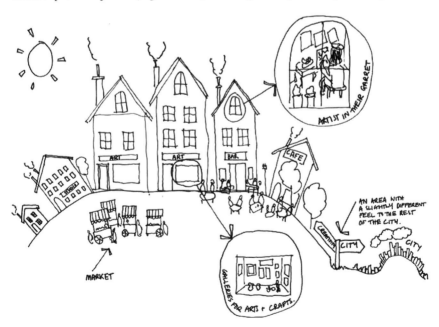

FIGURE 3.2.3 Gateshead Creative Quarter (archiGRAD's Thomas Ormerod).

documenting them at the outset of the project helps to improve communication in teamwork.

After that phase, the GRADs are then given one or two weeks in which to produce individual responses. The brief is deliberately loose at this stage, allowing the GRADs to respond to the shared information in a variety of ways. Facilitated by the mentors, individual ideas are discussed by the cohort and common or compatible ideas are identified for progression as a team proposal. Alternatively, individuals' responses are re-presented to show to the 'client' as options. The 'client's' feedback then informs the team's subsequent designs.

Identifying the potential

As the projects develop, we try to identify any implicit potential beyond fulfilling the 'client's' requirements in order to maximise the benefit for the participants and for the programme.

Projects with more proscribed outputs can offer GRADs opportunities to develop particular skills or, as in the case of community consultation and workshop activities, can develop 'tools' for future archiGRAD projects.

Self-generated briefs, such as the second cohort's 'Provocative Projects' or the perennial 'Unemployed Buildings', are explicitly intended to raise awareness of a particular issue, to demonstrate the GRADs' abilities to present creative (usually low-cost or reversible) solutions, and to promote the GRAD programme to potential 'clients' and future participants.

Maintaining momentum

To maintain focus and enthusiasm, projects have frequent deadlines of between one and three weeks. This also ensures that work is consolidated regularly, making it easier to keep the Design Report updated and allowing for the number of participants in each project to vary depending on their availability and the level of input required by each project at each stage.

GRADmag

GRADmag began as a means of encouraging the recording of work in progress and of documenting aspects of the participants' experiences which were not part of the projects (Figure 3.2.4). It was also intended to promote the programme to other unemployed graduates and students in their final years of study. Seven issues of GRADmag have been produced to date. From issue #3 (October 2011) onwards, GRADmag has been printed by National Building Specification (NBS). With their sponsorship, circulation of GRADmag has been extended to practices in the region.

Managing project documentation

Recording development work during a project is essential in managing projects whose groups' participants can change suddenly. It also ensures that any work

FIGURE 3.2.4 GRADmags.

produced is 'portfolio-ready' if participants are invited to an interview at short notice.

We have experienced an inherent resistance amongst architecture graduates to documenting their work adequately as it progresses. This appears to be perceived as a misuse of time that could be spent producing new work. The constant challenge is to ensure neither work in progress nor completed projects are 'lost', either because participants fail to 'back up' their files or to copy them to the archiGRAD hard drive before they leave the programme.

The need to 'back up' past and current work and each individual's contributions to ongoing projects has to be emphasised regularly at mentor meetings. This situation has been improved greatly with the use of Dropbox, a cloud-storage website, enabling current files to be shared by all participants between meetings. 'Backing up' completed projects from Dropbox is now managed following the mentor meetings; a protocol for maintaining functional free space on this site is becoming established.

Conclusion

During the RIBA's 'Love Architecture Festival 2013', archiGRAD staged their first independent exhibition in the Quillam Brothers' Teahouse in Newcastle. 'we are archiGRAD!', sponsored by Balfour Beatty, was seen by up to 1,456 visitors to the Teahouse. Curating this exhibition enabled us to reflect on the work produced over the first three years and on the number of GRADs who participated in shaping the GRAD programme.

archiGRAD is the catalyst for a geographically 'local cluster' (Kramer and Porter 2011) of architecture graduates and related disciplines. It demonstrates at least the possibility of a more agile and enterprising model of professional practice generated by a shared-value approach, able to collaborate with a network of peers on a project-by-project basis. Such a network would fulfil our original aspirations for the GRAD programme and would be a positive legacy of the current recession.

Notes

1   The Northern Architecture GRAD programme was founded by: Carol Botten, Director of Northern Architecture, the Architecture Centre for the North East (further information and contact details available at: http://www.northernarchitecture.com/home.html); Matthew Margetts, Director of +3 Architecture and Lecturer at Newcastle University (further information and contact details available at: http://www.plus3.co.uk/); Sebastian Messer RIBA, Senior Lecturer at Northumbria University (further information and contact details available at: http://www.northumbria.ac.uk/sd/academic/ee/staff/sebastian messer). Websites accessed January 2014.
2   PEDR provides evidence of completing the mandatory, minimum period of 24 months postgraduate work experience required by the Architects' Registration Board (ARB) and RIBA prior to taking the final examinations leading to registration as an architect in the UK. Further information available at: http://www.pedr.co.uk/Guide/StudentIntro Accessed January 2014.
3   *GUTS* by Peter Dillon (2013). Directed by Fiona MacPherson (The North East of England Institute of Mining and Mechanical Engineers' Mining Institute, Newcastle upon Tyne, 19 June). *GUTS* was staged during the Festival of the North East 2013.

References

archiGRAD (2013). Available online at: http://www.archiGRAD.co.uk Accessed January 2014.

Kramer, M. and Porter, M. (2011). 'Creating Shared Value'. *Harvard Business Review* Available online at: http://hbr.org/2011/01/the-big-idea-creating-shared-value Accessed January 2014.

Rajkovics, P. (2012). 'About Poaching!' In *Manual for Emerging Architects*, ed. S. Forlanti and A. Ispoo. Springer-Verlag, pp. 40–45.

Royal Institute of British Architects (2011). 'Host Practice'. Available online at: http://www.architecture.com/EducationAndCareers/CareersAndOpportunities/HostPractice/HostPractice.aspx#.UtLxM_tW-sg Accessed January 2014.

Royal Institute of British Architects (2009). 'RIBA Launches New Host Practice Scheme to Help Students'. Available online at: http://www.architecture.com/NewsAndPress/News/RIBANews/Press/2009/RIBALaunchHostPracticeScheme.aspx Accessed January 2014.

3.3

THE URBAN LAB

An experiment in education, research, and outreach

Beverly A. Sandalack

Introduction

The Urban Lab at the University of Calgary is an award-winning research group that deals with urban design, planning, and development issues, and is committed to Live Projects pedagogy. Established in 2000 as a means of providing intellectual direction to the emerging Urban Design Program, the Urban Lab sits between a traditional Community Design Center and an academic research institute, and connects sponsored urban-scale projects, student interns, and a design methodology derived from research.

Context: University of Calgary

The University of Calgary in Alberta, Canada, is located at the intersection of the prairies and the foothills. A young and prosperous city, Calgary is one of the country's fastest growing centers and the hub of a larger region that is experiencing all the challenges of western contemporary development. Planning, design, and development issues abound in this environment.

The Faculty of Environmental Design (EVDS) at the University of Calgary was established in 1971 as a graduate school for interdisciplinary design education, and currently has professional programs in architecture and planning and Masters and PhD degrees in environmental design. From 2002 to 2007 a separate field of study in urban design was offered which has since been advanced primarily through individual faculty efforts, notably the EVDS Urban Lab.

The Urban Lab was initiated by the author in 2000 to help define the intellectual direction of urban design studies in the faculty. It had some simple objectives: to bridge between the traditional academic research of the university and the practical needs of the community, to provide internship opportunities for graduate students,

FIGURE 3.3.1 Urban Lab staff.

and to be a vehicle through which a coherent urban design approach, appropriate to the Calgary context, could be developed and tested.

Mission and model

The Urban Lab does not conform to either the traditional Community Design Center model or the university research institute, although it has characteristics of each. Community Design Centers (CDCs) emerged during the 1950s and 1960s as planners, architects, and designers started to take on an advocacy role for otherwise underserved communities. Today, there are numerous CDCs in the US and a few in Canada, many located in universities that offer design and planning assistance to communities and non-profit groups. They combine teaching and training for students and, although they provide a product, the pedagogical process is emphasized (Spatial Agency 2014). In contrast, university research institutes (URIs) are groups of faculty and students concerned primarily with the discovery of new knowledge through research and the dissemination of the results; their work is typically funded by university or government grants. They may or may not have direct involvement with the community beyond the university, and may or may not be responding to community issues.

The Urban Lab is a hybrid between CDCs and URIs. It takes on projects that originate with community needs, but also seeks out more conventional research funding. Often the applied and pure research aspects are combined in one project. Although the Urban Lab responds to requests from civic groups, it makes clear that it is only interested in taking on projects that are not suitable for conventional professional planning and design consultants. Typically, these issues are not well defined and require a significant research component, and also may arise after conventional processes have not provided an appropriate solution. One of the selection criteria of Urban Lab community-based projects is that the scope of work must be collaboratively developed by funding and the research groups. In that way, each project contributes to knowledge and assists the community.

The Urban Lab has also led or participated in research projects that have been funded by conventional university or government grants. For these projects, the criteria include an applied aspect to the work, so that the knowledge can be furthered through urban design practice.

The combination of pure and applied research is essential. If the Lab did not take on Live Projects it could become a technical, abstract, and ultimately irrelevant endeavor; and if it did not pursue conventional research it could soon become formulaic and conventional, and be seen simply as a less-expensive alternative to conventional consulting.

Approach

Essentially, Urban Lab's approach pursues the improvement of human environments. This is informed by findings from conventional research published in books and academic journals, such as Sandalack *et al.*'s research on neighborhood form and walkability (in press). These findings are restated and refined through Live Projects. Urban Lab has also published ideas in the popular press to disseminate knowledge in a public forum (notably Sandalack and Dewald 2005–2008).

The approach and methodology used by the Urban Lab emphasizes three guiding principles: landscape and the public realm should be the organizing infrastructure of urban form (see Figure 3.3.2); sense of place should be supported; and community bonds should be strengthened. The principles have been applied and the methodology tested in projects of various scales. In each project, the Urban Lab is interested in finding new methods and tools for analysis, graphic communication, and design, and in integrating this work back into the teaching curriculum, resulting in a kind of institutional learning.

The conceptual diagram shown in Figure 3.3.2 (Sandalack and Nicolai 2006) illustrates the relationships of various components of the (ideal) built environment, and their degree of permanence:

- The land, and landscape character, is the most permanent aspect of the built environment and greatest contributor to a sense of place.
- Much of our everyday urban existence occurs within the shared city space: streets, sidewalks, parks, squares, and plazas. Collectively known as the public realm, it constitutes the next most permanent component of the built landscape.
- Several generations of built form come and go within the life cycle of the city; if the infrastructure of the public realm is intact, the built form has a sense of continuity and meaning over time.

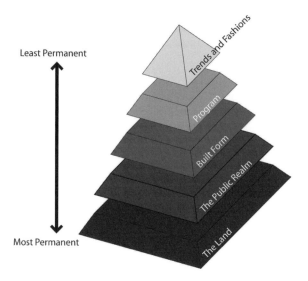

FIGURE 3.3.2 Conceptual diagram (from Sandalack and Nicolai 2006) illustrating the relationships of various components of the (ideal) built environment, and their degree of permanence.

- Each individual building, if its form is resilient, may be used for various programs. This robustness contributes to the sense of place through continuity of form.
- The least permanent aspects of the built environment, and of design activity, are ephemeral trends and fashions.

Pedagogy

An important objective of the Urban Lab is to provide opportunities for students to engage in Live Projects and to learn by doing. The pedagogical approach is based on the studio teaching model, where by graduate students are hired on a competitive basis and supervised by the author and a research associate, also an alumnus of EVDS. In most cases, students join the research group with only basic skills but strong potential and aptitude. The initial months focus on intense training. As the project and skills progress, students are given more latitude to develop their work and to provide insights into the overall research objectives. We attempt to involve students in as many aspects of the project as possible, exposing them within a short period of time to multiple project components. Even with strong oversight, the students are encouraged to think critically and analytically and to contribute to all project discussions. This model is very successful and has attracted more applicants than we have the capacity to employ.

Townscape analysis

Over time, a coherent approach known as townscape analysis was developed through research and project execution at various scales and locations (Kirby *et al.* 2003; Sandalack and Nicolai 1998). It utilizes techniques and methods from urban morphology, landscape architecture, urban design, and urban planning; depends on multiple sources of primary information; and is conducted at various inter-related scales. Documentation and analysis normally include:

a. Environmental analysis: an inventory of topography, hydrology, geology, vegetation, and so on, and their inter-relationships, over time, on regional and local levels (McHarg 1969; Forman and Godron 1986).
b. Land uses and functional relationships: an analysis of a town or city's spatial structure considering land utilization and the pattern of activities, and the location and distribution of uses and their functional relationships (Lynch 1960), analyzed in terms of their historical evolution.
c. Morphology, typology, and visual relationships: urban form analysis based on the three-dimensional qualities of lots, blocks, streets, buildings, and open spaces, over time, including their relationship with each other (Moudon 1997), using lot subdivision, figure-ground mapping, air photo analysis, and historical evolution studies. It includes typological studies and visual analyses.
d. Public engagement: consideration of the knowledge, opinions, aspirations and perceptions of the residents, and of those who are involved in making and managing the built environment. This might include surveys, questionnaires, visual preference exercises, mapping exercises, the use of 3D physical and digital models for visualization of options, and so on.

Project examples

A single project with a modest budget dealing with Calgary's emerging cultural district began in 2000. Over time, more internal grants and outside contracts (approximately $1.5 million CAD thus far) were secured. More than forty-five student internships have been funded to date, and three professional research associates have had full-time employment through projects, providing project management, mentoring, supervision, and preparation for publication.

The following projects are some of those included (in order of physical scale).

Cliff Bungalow-Mission Townscape and Process (2001) (Figure 3.3.3) arose in response to the city's interest in an alternative to the Area Redevelopment Plan process for established communities. The process included building types analysis and lessons learned about the inter-relationships of scales.

Calgary Cultural District – A Framework for the Future (2000) (Figure 3.3.4) introduced initiatives to strengthen this district. We experimented with ways of documenting and analyzing use patterns, including permeability analysis.

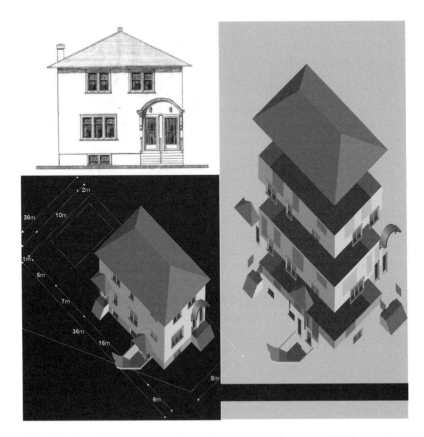

FIGURE 3.3.3 Cliff Bungalow-Mission Townscape and Process (2001) arose in response to the city's interest in an alternative to the Area Redevelopment Plan process for established communities.

Benalto Area Redevelopment Plan (2006) (Figure 3.3.5) provided concepts for a small hamlet, illustrated in the perspective sketch shown in Figure 3.3.5. Approachable drawings and models were emphasized.

Red Deer County Open Space Master Plan (2009) (Figure 3.3.6) was a multi-year project involving specialized mapping and analysis of an area of 1,500 square miles, including public consultation, documentation of physical/cultural landscapes, assessment of issues and opportunities, and several scales of design. This project showed the value of long-term projects in achieving community and pedagogic goals.

In addition to multiple projects, several books based on the work's research aspects have been published, including *Making Better Civic Places: Urban Design at the University of Calgary*, a compendium of projects (Kirby *et al.* 2003); *The Calgary Project: Urban Form/Urban Life*, which is now used as a teaching tool (Sandalack and Nicolai 2006); and two books arising from the Sense of Place project (a series of

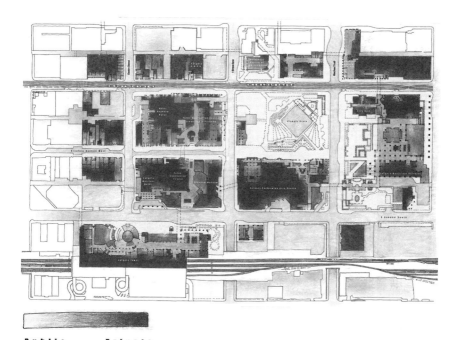

Public **Private**

FIGURE 3.3.4 Calgary Cultural District – A Framework for the Future (2000).

FIGURE 3.3.5 Benalto Area Redevelopment Plan, perspective sketch (2006).

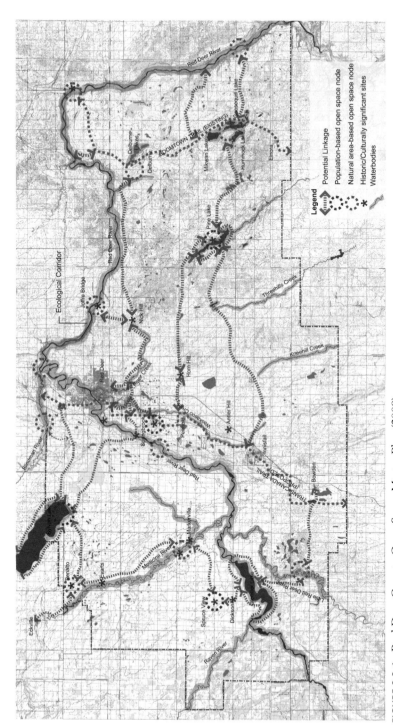

FIGURE 3.3.6 Red Deer County Open Space Master Plan (2009).

events and exhibitions celebrating Alberta's Centennial), which then became the basis for new courses (Davis and Sandalack 2005; Sandalack and Davis 2005).

When evaluating projects we ask several questions: How well did the project respond to our underlying principles? Did the project include meaningful public engagement that educated residents and strengthened community bonds? Does the project make a useful contribution to our teaching? Did the students employed as research assistants increase their skills, knowledge, and design process? Does the project contribute to new knowledge or better practice? How do our peers evaluate our work through awards and publications?

Summary

The Live Projects model allows teaching, training, and education to evolve in real time, while making concrete contributions to the community and our academic programs. The experience of the Urban Lab over the past thirteen years has demonstrated the value of Live Projects for their contributions to knowledge and practice and their effectiveness in providing exceptional educational experiences for students and alumni.

Despite the many benefits of the Urban Lab, there have been a number of issues. University processes and protocols do not always recognize Urban Lab projects as "legitimate" research, and every project grant requires justification and negotiation. Funding is a constant effort, since the Lab operates on a project-to-project basis. Direction comes from only one full-time faculty member, making the endeavor vulnerable in some ways; efforts to expand and institutionalize the role of the Research Associate through regular teaching have thus far been unsuccessful.

Despite the inability of the university to easily accommodate the unique characteristics of the Urban Lab, it persists. The Lab provides a unique learning setting between the classroom and the workplace; students are taught skills beyond their courses and given increasing responsibility within the context of the project constraints and they are also expected to develop professional accountabilities and attitudes (if within the pedagogical support of the university setting).

Students working as interns learn about many inter-related aspects of planning and design and acquire skills in analysis, design, and working with the public, as well as graphic and other communication skills. Positions in the Lab are highly sought after, and students who are hired for projects also frequently serve as teaching assistants in planning and urban design courses.

Contact with real-world problems is a part of our academic programs, and in professional programs it is even more essential for practice to inform teaching. This cannot be done in the classroom alone – the practice of urban design depends on Live Projects. Equally important is the political role that the Urban Lab (and units like it) plays in influencing theory, practice, and action through Live Projects.

Acknowledgements

Calgary Cultural District: A Framework for the Future: Cultural District Partnership; Regional Citation, Canadian Society of Landscape Architects (CSLA).

Cliff Bungalow-Mission Area Redevelopment Plan: Calgary Foundation; National Merit and Regional Honour, CSLA.

Benalto Concept Plan: Red Deer County; National Honour, CSLA.

The Calgary Project: urban form/urban life: University of Calgary and ENMAX Power; National Honour, CSLA.

Red Deer County Open Space Master Plan: with Dillon Consulting Ltd; Red Deer County; Merit Award, Alberta Professional Planners Institute; Regional Citation, CSLA; Award of Excellence, Recreation Alberta.

Sense of Place series of events: with the Nickle Arts Museum; University of Calgary and the Alberta Lotteries Foundation; National Honour, CSLA; Place Planning Award, Environmental Design Research Association; Calgary Heritage Award.

References

Davis, A. and Sandalack, B.A. (eds) (2005). *Sense of Place*. Nickle Arts Museum.

Forman, R.T.T. and Godron, M. (1986). *Landscape Ecology*. Wiley.

Kirby, R., Nicolai, A., and Sandalack, B.A. (2003). *Making Better Civic Places: Urban Design at the University of Calgary*. Faculty of Environmental Design.

Lynch, K. (1960). *The Image of the City*. MIT Press.

McHarg, I. (1969, reissued 1992). *Design with Nature*. Natural History Press.

Moudon, A.V. (1997). 'Urban Morphology as an Emerging Interdisciplinary Field'. *Urban Morphology*, 1: 3–10.

Sandalack, B.A., and Davis, A. (eds) (2005). *Excursions into the Cultural Landscapes of Alberta*. Nickle Arts Museum.

Sandalack, B.A., and Dewald, J. (2005–2008). *Calgary Herald Column*. Available online at: http://www.ucalgary.ca/urbanlab/node/77 Accessed January 2014.

Sandalack, B.A., and Nicolai, A. (1998). *Urban Structure – Halifax: An Urban Design Approach*. TUNS Press.

Sandalack, B.A., and Nicolai, A (2006). *The Calgary Project: Urban Form/Urban Life*. University of Calgary Press.

Sandalack, B.A., Alaniz Uribe, F., Eshghzadeh, A., Shiell, A., McCormack, G.R., and Doyle-Baker, P.K. (in press). 'Neighbourhood Type and Walkshed Size'. *Journal of Urbanism*.

Spatial Agency (2014). Available online at: http://www.spatialagency.net/ Accessed January 2014.

3.4

A PEDAGOGICAL GAP

Barnaby Bennett and Ryan Reynolds

As a professional graduate degree, architecture has long held a tension between the need to train people in a discipline for a specific occupation and the more traditional liberal role of the university as a site for critical reflection on society. Increasingly, the latter option is unavailable to students and teachers alike, even in the liberal arts, which pioneered the notion that the ability to critique and think outside the norms of society is essential for the formation of active citizens. This chapter therefore considers to what extent Live Projects can facilitate critical reflection in aspiring architects.

Live Projects as pedagogical opportunity

In 1972 Simon Nicholson published his theory of loose parts as a political attack on the 'lie . . . that the planning, design and building of *any part* of the environment is so difficult and so special that only the gifted few – those with degrees and certificates in planning, engineering, architecture, art, education, behavioural psychology and so on – can properly solve environmental problems' (1972: 5). Most people, he argues, *receive* the built environment as a finished whole for them to use or inhabit but get no chance to experiment themselves with the components and variables of the world.

Live Projects have contradictory potential: as real-world experiments for non-professionals, through generally small-scale, self-sufficient, and self-directed projects, to make truly original (and therefore threatening to the status quo) social and cultural interventions; and as training exercises for would-be experts to develop their (exclusive) mastery over the built environment. Following Nicholson, we are interested in the radical and innovative potential of genuine public experimentation.

Emergency and crisis

Like Live Projects, disasters – natural or man-made; physical, economic, or cultural – give rise to contradictory responses, needs, and desires. Disasters open up the need for immediate practical responses to restore some functional level of normality, but also create space (and time) where autonomy is possible and even necessary, as the 'system' – the normal hierarchies – cannot cope and people must temporarily fend for themselves until order is re-established.

Architect Mark Wigley makes a distinction between emergency and crisis that is useful for exploring the above tension:

> A crisis is the moment that the threat is not just inside the space but is actually an extreme challenge to the space itself. ... If an emergency is a threat within a system, a crisis is a threat to the whole system. ... In a crisis, things spin out of scale and therefore out of control. ... Crises always appear as the failure of a spatial system, a failure of architecture. It is no longer simply a damaged spatial system needing emergency care. Something has so radically lost its shape that it cannot be repaired. ... Nobody can plan for crisis since crisis is exactly the name for that which defeats both planning beforehand and response afterwards.
>
> *(Wigley 2009: 6)*

According to this distinction, *crises* are situations where a practical conservative response, repairing the damaged system, no longer makes sense or is no longer possible. For this reason a crisis represents a threat to the status quo and can be used as a political weapon. To call something a crisis is not a statement of fact; it's an allegation, an accusation, and as such a deeply political act. To say something is in crisis is to challenge it, to destabilize it, to question its validity.

Post-quake Christchurch

As workplaces reopened and old routines were reinstated in the weeks and months following the major earthquakes, Christchurch residents overwhelmingly reported that the quakes had had some positive effects and people were – in a sense – sad to see such a quick return to a 'new normal'. In the immediate aftermath residents had (re)discovered a sense of neighbourliness, community, generosity, and self-reliance that was not often experienced in society and was arguably threatening to dominant cultural hierarchies. This observation is seemingly common in the wake of disasters worldwide (see Solnit 2009). There is a tension, then, between the strong desire for a return to familiarity and the strong desire to experience and explore new social values and possibilities – a parallel tension to that between Wigley's 'emergency' and 'crisis'.

The Live Projects that have been emerging in this semi-autonomous space–time have the opportunity to respond to both desires: the restoration of immediate amenity and the pursuit of a (new) longer-term stability based on different values. Some of the works consciously engage with both, and use the opportunity not only to meet immediate needs but also to participate in imaginative (potentially system-changing) city building exercises.

Gap Filler and others

After the first big quake in September 2010 an informal group comprising an architect, two performers, a visual artist, a designer, and a project manager emerged to run creative projects on the (20-some) vacant city sites where buildings had collapsed or been demolished. The name, Gap Filler, perhaps evidences their thinking that this initiative was in response to an 'emergency', and that there was a need to provide temporary amenity and attraction while the old system was being repaired.

After the far more damaging quake in February 2011 the organization was revised and expanded. The name remains the same, but the published philosophy now evidences a desire to collectively reimagine what the city could be 'by actually doing it, not just talking about it' (Winn 2013). Such concrete reimagining seems much more aligned to a perceived state of 'crisis' in which the return of the old system seems no longer feasible or desired. Gap Filler now has a large following in the city and a strong media presence, and has helped give rise to other organizations and initiatives that amount to an alternative movement in the city, trying to inaugurate a new social logic.

Projects to date – by Gap Filler and others – have included volunteer-built temporary community venues, public wood-fired pizza ovens, a temporary hand-built sweatlodge, free outdoor cinemas, community gardens, a dance floor with

FIGURE 3.4.1 Gap Filler office.

DIY jukebox, and much more. They seem driven by the desire to articulate a new social logic, but it is of course possible (even probable) that, in the bigger picture, these projects will in fact support the status quo, acting as temporary outlets for people's potentially revolutionary energy until the old system reasserts itself. Put another way, these projects are part of a struggle over whether Christchurch is in a state of emergency, awaiting repair, or a state of crisis that requires reimagining – and 'gaps' have seemingly become space–times where the progressive logic of crisis is preserved. The contestable nature of crisis entails that the lessons from this post-disaster setting could be made relevant in other contexts, where 'gaps' – certain space–times – can be produced, through behaviours, as temporary autonomous zones.

Gaps as pedagogical opportunity?

Live Projects can be used to develop professional skills and/or to enable the development of critical consciousness, which can be seen to parallel the distinction between emergency and crisis. Producing spaces (times) for Live Projects that are in-between emergency and crisis creates a two-fold pedagogical opportunity. Students exercise their skills by responding to immediate social needs but are forced to consider the broader political consequences of these actions; or, the needs of the city are met by improvised and experimental actions necessitated and constrained by the situation. In short, Live Projects in 'gaps' can re-create or replace lost amenity and (perhaps simultaneously) create an ethically informed alternative.

We will briefly look at two case studies. While both are deeply embedded in the complex situation of Christchurch, they should each have aspects that transcend that context and indicate how similar tactics could be used in other contexts for similar pedagogical outcomes.

Think Differently Book Exchange

The closure of the main public library in the city removed an important civic and social space. A temporarily unemployed librarian suggested the creation of a book exchange. Gap Filler secured an empty glass-doored commercial refrigerator and placed it, and a bench, on an empty city site near the old library. They held a launch event, inviting members of the public to donate books 'that had made them think differently' to stock the fridge – and then left it on the site, where it could be used by anyone 24 hours a day.

The social experiment is enhanced by the books themselves, which arguably become the loose parts that enable a different logic to develop. Liberated from the conventional security and ownership model, they become part of a new system based on generosity, trust, and community maintenance. This month-long experiment was so embraced by the public (and landowner) that it has now been running for more than two years.

FIGURE 3.4.2   Think Differently Book Exchange by Gap Filler.

Luxcity/FESTA

The largest example of student involvement was the opening night event of the inaugural Festival of Transitional Architecture: Luxcity. More than 350 architecture, interior design, and spatial architecture students from around the country worked with local artists and businesses to temporarily activate one downtown street for a night. The students, from Christchurch Polytechnic, University of Auckland, Victoria University of Wellington, Unitec, and Auckland University of Technology, worked on fourteen large architectural installations 'made of light' that enabled the delivery of a massive festival (with 20,000 attendees) in the midst of the central city ruin on a very small budget.

For many residents, this event (nineteen months on from the big quake) was the first occasion on which they revisited the central city. The same cranes that were being used to demolish buildings were employed for this weekend to suspend the architectural installations and give them a colossal scale – permitting residents to reimagine a thriving city, an urban scale, and an architecture not rooted in weight and permanence.

FIGURE 3.4.3 Luxcity, Festival of Transitional Architecture (FESTA), Christchurch New Zealand, 2012.

FIGURE 3.4.4 Luxcity, Festival of Transitional Architecture (FESTA), Christchurch New Zealand, 2012.

FIGURE 3.4.5 Luxcity, Festival of Transitional Architecture (FESTA), Christ-church New Zealand, 2012.

Conclusion

In this chapter we have tried to express how the crises that develop after disaster are as much the symptom of a system's inability to cope with change as they are a result of the disaster itself. Crisis demands a response, but is also an implicit critique of what was before. Indeed, the words *crisis* and *critical* are both etymologically derived from the Greek word *krinein*, meaning 'able to discern' or 'judge'.

By purposefully reimagining ways of living while responding to the practical needs of a city in crisis this ability to discern is developed. Critical thought is enabled by the crisis, explicitly via making interventions. In fact, it may be the Live Projects themselves that identify that there is a crisis, as opposed to an emergency. Students and the city are able to enter into meaningful experimentation that is neither too dangerous nor too safe.

Common to the two examples above is that their realization is very pub-lic and involves a certain amount of improvisation in this open setting. This demonstration of reasonably communal design and construction shows that the public can experiment, at least in relatively small ways, with the loose parts of the city and its spatial design. This, at its core, is the system-changing logic that sits alongside the restored amenity: that the city can be created by and for the public living in it rather than (solely) by experts, planners, and economists. Exploring this circumstance is the unique pedagogical opportunity of 'gaps'.

We, as educators and designers, need to be awake to the danger of this pedagog-ical position becoming the opposite of what it is intended to be. If we focus energy primarily on the benefits of Live Projects to designers and our discipline we risk institutionalizing knowledge and supplanting the creative potential of communities with our own frames and ideas of the world.

References

Fukuyama, Francis (1992). *The End of History and the Last Man*. Free Press.

Nicholson, Simon (1972). 'The Theory of Loose Parts: An Important Principle for Design Methodology'. *Studies in Design Education Craft and Technology*, 4(2): 5–14.

Solnit, Rebecca (2009). *A Paradise Built in Hell: The Extraordinary Communities that Arise in Disaster*. Penguin Books.

Wigley, Mark (2009). 'Space in Crisis'. *Volume Magazine*, Bootleg Edition Urban China (C-Lab), 19: 2–7.

Winn, Coralie (2013). *About Gap Filler*. Available online at: http://www.gapfiller.org.nz/about/Accessed January 2014.

3.5

ARCHITECTURAL EDUCATION BEYOND AN ACADEMIC CONTEXT

Christian Volkmann

Introduction

Any kind of education should suggest a field of professional application. In architecture, defined as the art and science of building, the skills learned in school are often not sufficient to prepare for typical professional activities. Although conceptual thinking, history-theory, or social sciences are all significant, one of the supposedly mandatory elements, *to materialize the imagined*, is often absent from the curriculum.

How can design teaching strategies make students aware of the need for an intertwined skill set that encompasses intellectual and practical components? What will motivate them to engage in hands-on practices that can develop sophisticated materialization skills for their future professional lives? How can we bring practical skills back into an academic field, where they have been neglected during past decades in favor of a "higher world of art, politics and philosophy" (Sennett 2009)?

The inevitable changes ahead, especially those related to the energy revolution in the building sector, will make hands-on implementation skills even more essential to impacting our socio-cultural environment. The emerging field opens opportunities to redefine the architectural profession as one that specializes in prototyping and implementation.

Preconditions

In Europe, the architect is often more involved in organizing a building project's construction logistics than in the United States. Seldom in the US is organizational negotiation with tradespeople within the architect's scope, but instead to a great extent resides with the General Contractor. The architect is more and more removed from tangible materialization.

As a consequence, many different professional niches have formed within architecture: one end of the spectrum focuses on virtual, two-dimensional representations of conceptual ideas, not intended for building; the other resides in functionary construction facilitation as a means to an end for the building industry. It is not often that these niches are combined to let design ambitions and means of construction serve each other in a meaningful way. But exactly this capability has to be fostered to create fully literate architects.

"Solar Roofpod" – starting point

When our school, the City College of New York (CCNY), became a finalist in the 2011 Solar Decathlon, a competition organized by the US Department of Energy (DOE) in which 20 selected college teams are awarded $100,000 to design, build, and exhibit "Net-Zero-Energy" houses on the National Mall in Washington, DC, the transfer of competencies between drawn and built architecture became my primary teaching objective.

In its mission statement, CCNY represents itself as "the school of the urban environment." Thus, we thematized the applications of urban sustainable strategies as laid out in New York City's PlaNYC (http://www.nyc.gov/html/planyc2030/html/home/home.shtml Accessed January 2014) and combined them with the competition brief. We invented the concept of the "Solar Roofpod" for New York's underutilized roofscape, which has the highest environmental loads and is also desired prime real estate.

FIGURE 3.5.1   "Solar Roofpod Utopia": vision of a future urban environment, taking advantage of the underutilized roofscape of New York City. (Student rendering.)

Over roughly eighteen months the conceptual idea of the "Solar Roofpod" was, under my guidance as program manager, translated into a built project. Beginning with studio work by two groups of 16 students, it was developed by students with shifting foci and subgroup configurations during the planning process, similar to those seen in a professional office, and culminated over a summer in physically constructing the building, excepting only phases requiring professional licensing.

Design pedagogy: methodology

Compelling design pedagogy must combine the ephemeral and the concrete. The students understood early that the *visionary* idea could only be as good as its *concrete* realization. Understanding the project not only as a drawn whole but also as an interconnected assembly of subsystems and tasks was crucial in the design process. This idea was discussed repeatedly, from the *whole* to its *parts* as well as from the *parts* to the *whole*: both directions had to be dealt with simultaneously.

Identifying the Roofpod's prototypical character forced us to intertwine diverse requirements: materials and products, prefabrication and assembly methods, customization concepts, load calculations and structural conditions, code issues, energy-efficiency analysis, material science, integration of renewables-based mechanical and electrical systems, budgetary, labor, and time constraints, and, not least, the organization of the corresponding set of drawings comprised most of the design activities. Thus, the project itself, and creating architecture in general, was understood differently.

The learning process reflected real-life design processing, using practical and cognitive skills within a social context. The project calibration within these forces improved the project, although not along a linear academic process ("this is what I want"), but rather through a negotiative set of rules ("this is what is feasible, under a certain set of conditions") more common to the profession. Design iterations

FIGURE 3.5.2 Chinese puzzle as pedagogic paradigm: artifacts have to be designed in both directions, from the "whole" to its "parts" as well as from the "parts" to the "whole."

processed concrete and realizable materialization strategies based on interdependent factors.

The negotiation process gave me a new understanding of teaching design studio. A set of goals cannot solely be based on an invented declaration, whose consequential logic is often explored only theoretically (frequently by heavily editing what deviates from the narrative), but, instead, should draw on a process of developing an "elegant consensus" among multiple interests and real, sometimes contradictory, criteria. Readiness for professional problem-solving is dependent on intellectual negotiation learned in school. "Comprehensive design" is thus of higher value to the profession than simplistic conceptual thinking.

In order to satisfy not only practical but also intellectual development, the connection between the mundane and the concrete is crucial: the reflection of the socio-cultural environment we serve and belong to must be the starting point of any intellectual investigation. If this component is understated, the realization process reverts to dull technology in a vacuum. The careful instrumentation of comprehensive design criteria, intellectual as well as practical, is thus vital for a successful project.

Teamwork

One of the most productive drivers of the project was the work in groups. The student groups were first brought together through my assignments to address building subsystems and task distribution, but later configured naturally through common interest, friendship, and gained expertise.

The teamwork had several benefits. Cognitive design decisions were double-checked when reflected upon with others. Diverse backgrounds led to productive discussions and better design decisions. A similar ambience is found in office environments: teamwork prepares communication skills and leads to more effective collaboration.

Determining individual semester grades was not an issue. Since the pragmatic research on materials and construction systems required individual follow-up, these tasks were assigned regularly and discussed in the subsequent sessions. These assignments were, however, more dynamic than usual studio teaching and needed constant adjustment. The students were also better aware of their performance, since these tasks were monitored and observed by their peers.

The students enjoyed having real decisions in their own hands and became better at evaluating criteria. They were, for example, responsible for in-kind fundraising and/or choosing labor-intensive, often cost-reducing materialization methods to achieve the level of quality and detail to which they aspired. They grew more sensitive to these topics as they experienced the associated efforts first hand. In the end, we fundraised $200,000; additional hours of physical labor were uncountable.

Since decisions were made jointly and publicly, the motivation and effort to reach the goals articulated were high.

Hands-on learning

In order to develop the skills necessary to understand material and assembly processes, hands-on electives for woodworking and metalwork, taught by professional
craftsmen, were coupled with design studio work. Mock-ups were built, resulting
in an ingenious "building block" envelope system as well as the cabinetry, railing
posts, ramps, porches, and other custom touches to the design. The intellectual
overlap between design studio and these courses was paramount to developing the
students' understanding of the relevance of practical knowledge for construction
documentation. A full comprehension of assembly sequences and tolerances was
formed; since these topics have no immediate consequences, they are difficult to
teach in drawings.

Teamwork skills, this time as fabricators, were also honed for the upcoming
construction. All the students understood their interdependence in realizing their
carefully planned architecture. When construction started several foremen of critical
trades (carpentry, roofing, electrical, mechanical, plumbing) regularly visited the
site to discuss necessary tasks and methods. The students were eager to learn from
these sources and incorporated the know-how gained.

Logistics: financing and public relations

The high financial burden of design–build projects has been criticized. The pressure
during the procurement phase of our project was severe. The scope, defined by the
DOE, might have been overambitious for an academic project. However, several

FIGURE 3.5.3 Experiencing construction, learning by doing. After instruction
from professionals, the students completed most of the building assembly themselves. Teamwork was crucial.

FIGURE 3.5.4 OPEN House. Upon completion, sponsors, press, and student families celebrated the finished product on campus. The involvement of the college's administration, especially Development and Public Relations offices, was important to the project's success.

strategies could be applied to secure similar, but down-scaled, projects in the future, as detailed below.

A holistic PR strategy is mandatory for a long-term design–build curriculum: the fact that we were sponsored by the Department of Energy's Solar Decathlon event, with 350,000 visitors on the National Mall, was persuasive for sponsors (industry, fabricators, alumni). It is thus important to build public presence, find partners for projects, and involve communities throughout the process.

Possible future projects with community boards neighboring our campus to create street or park components, or industry collaborations with manufacturers, have already been discussed. What all potential initiatives would have in common is a precisely defined and permanently maintained communication concept, with website(s), public events, exhibits, and publication presence.

We are also fortunate to have received a financial gift with an endowment dedicated to design–build pedagogy. The efficient involvement and commitment of the Development and Public Relations offices is thus paramount for long-term success.

Student survey – outcome

Although I was convinced that this project had changed the participants' understanding of their future professions, I still needed proof of my subjective observations. Even though the responses to central questions of materialization and project management had evolved dramatically, the intellectual impact on their self-conception as aspiring architects had to be surveyed more systematically. To this

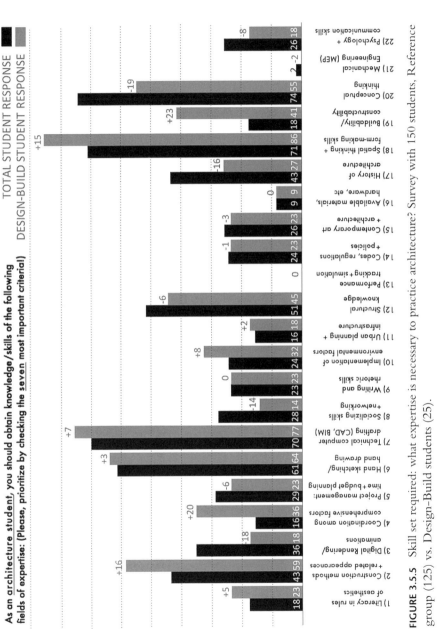

FIGURE 3.5.5 Skill set required: what expertise is necessary to practice architecture? Survey with 150 students, Reference group (125) vs. Design–Build students (25).

end, a reference group of around 150 students, among them 25 of my "design–build students," were asked to rank the most important skills an architect should have, and compare them against their own preferences as students.

It became apparent that both my design–build students and the reference group believed that professional and academic skill sets (professional architect vs. student) should differ, predominantly owing to students' interest in experimentation and intellectual development. However, the two groups developed completely different areas of emphasis in both their professional and academic skill set priorities. Focusing on the areas with the most pronounced differences between the two groups, the following result emerged: in the professional area (being an architect), the reference group emphasized "conceptual thinking" and "technical drafting (BIM, CAD)," while the design–build students identified "buildability" and "spatial thinking + form-making skills" as the far more crucial items. In the academic realm (being an architecture student), again "conceptual thinking" and "digital rendering" were emphasized by the reference group to a comparatively high percentage, while the design–build students chose "coordination among comprehensive factors" and, again, "buildability" as their crucial criteria. Other items valued by design–build students were "construction methods and related appearances" and "implementation of environmental factors," while the reference group favored "socializing skills and networking" and "history of architecture" as their target skills.

Survey conclusions

It is obvious that the activities preferred by the reference group are more theoretical (often emphasizing abstract means of representation), while the subjects preferred by the design–build students were more practically oriented and negotiative, often related to concrete requirements that arose as they developed the Roofpod project. The effect the project had is thus evident in the survey: the Roofpod cohort chose skills needed "to materialize the imagined."

These skills lead to a more literate practitioner. The capabilities gained during the Roofpod project will significantly contribute to abilities used when teamwork and negotiation skills are mandatory to implement a conceptual idea. To promote these vital competencies and capitalize on practical problem-solving and hands-on materialization, academic curricula must be enriched with design–build projects.

Broader pedagogic perspectives

It is clear that certain design skills can only be learned if material processing is experienced haptically and motorically. In Bloom's taxonomy (Bloom 1956; Simpson 1972), the domain associated with acquiring motoric skills is described as the "psychomotor": this kind of learning, necessary to process the complexities of built assemblies, cannot be acquired by drawing, but needs physical attention (see also

FIGURE 3.5.6 Reassembly of the "Solar Roofpod" on the National Mall, Washington DC, September 2011; the students had gained confidence in understanding the whole building after having experienced the pieces and methods necessary to complete it.

Figure 3.5.2). Know-how in architecture and material-based fields in general is based on experiential learning (Kolb 1984) and repetitive processing.

Broadening the impact of "design–build" learning depends on its placement in the curriculum. How can a holistic plan be developed that sequences courses to promote practical material processing, from simple assignments to more advanced projects? Haptic realization must be repeated in the curriculum. Early on, simple material systems could be developed, while, at the end of the academic sequence, when advanced comprehensive thinking is evolved, a small building, suitable for systems integration and including attention to social and budgetary conditions, among other generative factors, should be incorporated into an advanced project. The development of design skills should begin with basic architectural design drivers, such as space, light, context, and so on, and amalgamate increasingly towards comprehensive criteria related to everyday professional design practice. The academic mission is creative comprehensive thinking as a performative skill.

As evident in the terminal projects of other professions, such as the cabinetmaker's "masterpiece" at the end of a traditional apprenticeship, the testing and comprehensive use of knowledge demonstrates the ability to transition into a creative and prolific professional occupation, also facilitating interdisciplinary collaboration and social engagement.

Design–build: architectural research

Finally, it is important that the students (as shown in the survey) realize their own shift towards a more tangible profession. Design–build projects can be considered research in architectural materialization. In past decades many available building systems have been streamlined by industry. As a result, the majority of building production has become more repetitive and unimaginative. If hands-on processing skills were lost when developing architectural assemblies, this deficiency would certainly worsen. The outcome would be a loss of originality in our built environment.

One of the main reasons why many students initially shied away from our Solar Roofpod project (and more practical efforts in general) is anxiety about failure, which is more apparent in built than in just drawn projects. Teachers must apply encouragement to overcome these insecurities in the field of concrete materialization. "Prototyping," as material-based designing, should be considered research, and thus must utilize trial and error. Research clearly depends on originality: errors are part of the risk-taking process, necessary to develop something extraordinary. In the end, the students' confidence will hold the greatest power to change the culture of their profession.

References

Bloom, Benjamin (1956). *Taxonomy of Educational Objectives: The Classification of Educational Goals; Handbook 1: Cognitive Domain.* Longmans Green.

Kolb, David A. (1984). *Experiential Learning: Experience as the Source of Learning and Development.* Prentice Hall.

Sennett, Richard (2009). *The Craftsman.* Yale University Press.

Simpson, Elizabeth J. (1972). *The Classification of Educational Objectives in the Psychomotor Domain.* Gryphon House.

Volkmann, Christian (2013). *Prototyping Architecture: The Solar Roofpod – An Educational Design–build Research Project.* Oscar Riera Ojeda Publ.

PART IV

Case studies

4.1

CONSTRUCTING A CONTINGENT PEDAGOGY

Michael Hughes

Introduction

Traditional architectural skills such as spatial cognition and formal composition are well honed in the normative academic design studio. However, the professional skills associated with negotiating the stress-filled reality of complex, collaborative projects defined by teams of consultants and multiple, often mutually exclusive, variables are difficult to model in an academic setting.

Building on the example education known as design–build in North America, and Live Projects in Europe, this chapter outlines the challenges and latent opportunities encountered in the ongoing development of an immersive approach to the full scope of architectural education. In this effort, contingency, understood as the unforeseen and uncontrollable aspects of architectural practice, is being foregrounded as a primary, fundamental teaching tool. Ultimately, the goal is to empower students with the instrumental agency and improvisational intelligence necessary to navigate the unknown, and unknowable, that defines all real-world endeavors.

Messy reality

The full-scale, hands-on approach exemplified by design–build education provides a potential venue for direct encounter with contingency within an academic environment. Embracing the contingent character of contemporary architectural practice would introduce students to a complex and realistic realm of inter-personal and inter-professional dependence. In this context simultaneous engagement with multiple variables develops improvisational skills that hone decision-making skills.

In the face of these challenges, learning opportunities involving complexity are often artificially curtailed by imposed limits. Lead faculty tend to limit the project scope and take on the bulk of logistical preparations in order to allow students to focus on some sub-set of reality, most often the design and build aspects, and ultimately to increase the likelihood of an "on-time" project completion.

Pushing students to learn beyond the walls of the university through design–build projects imparts important practical lessons that are difficult to convey through traditional studio-based methods. However, the exposure is often limited by the coordinating faculty to engage a partial, abstracted field of operation, carefully orchestrated to focus on specific variables to the exclusion of complicating or messy reality – clients, project procurement, budget, codes, and so on.

Case study 01: the Tectonic Landscape Initiative

Most of the projects completed through the ongoing Tectonic Landscapes Initiative, such as TrailerWrap and the Outdoor Classroom, have followed the design–build model of careful orchestration. As those involved were intent on completing the projects on time and on budget, external, contingent conditions, including clients, were often seen as intrusive and disruptive. On the surface, this may sound like an indictment of the design–build model. In fact, it is a reasonable response to an unreasonable context. As previously mentioned, the logistical challenges faced by faculty in the design–build model are substantial and often unrecognized.

Of all the variables conspiring against full-immersion pedagogies, the academic calendar is one of the most insidious. Administrators define faculty teaching loads and student course loads in terms of fifteen-week semesters and credit hours, but architectural projects, especially those completed by students, resist this structure. The Rural Studio at Auburn University has taken what many would see as a radical

FIGURE 4.1.1   TrailerWrap. Boulder, CO, 2004–2006.

FIGURE 4.1.2 FORM/work. Albuquerque, NM, 1998–1999.

approach to resolving the conflict between academic calendars and project time-lines. Students admitted to the fifth-year thesis work in small teams and all team members agree to commit to a single project for the entire duration. As a result, students are exposed to the full spectrum of the endeavor, but the projects often extend across multiple semesters and even years. For example, the widely published Newbern Fire Station project lasted over two years.[1]

Case study 02: the Outdoor Classroom

The Outdoor Classroom project serves to illustrate some of the potential lessons typically hidden from the students' view and/or participation in design–build pedagogy.

For this project negotiations included six primary stakeholders: the municipality, which governed building codes and license enforcement; the school district, which owned the site; the non-profit parent organization, which provided the funding; the university, which provided the design–build team; the teachers and students, who

FIGURE 4.1.3   Outdoor Classroom. Fayetteville, AR, 2007–2008.

represented the immediate user group; and the adjacent neighbors, who represented a broader community coalition. Coordination and negotiation among these groups required the faculty member in charge to facilitate the efforts of four lawyers and totaled six months of effort before students started the design–build phase.

The preparatory phase began nine months before students began the project and included negotiations internal to the university. The Dean of the college, the department head, and the faculty member had to agree on the schedule, teaching load equivalency, contingency plans, and teaching/research/service implications. The college and the university then worked together to structure legal agreements, determine risk-management protocols, locate campus facilities, identify mentors within the campus maintenance office and create agreements for their participation, develop funding strategies, and streamline accounting procedures. The lead faculty member was solely responsible for all of this coordination and preparation.

The Outdoor Classroom also involved three separate groups of students across three semesters. There was no continuity save for the faculty member. As a result students were not exposed to the logistical challenges and the faculty member bore the responsibility alone.

Case study 03: PORCH_house prefab

In contrast to the Outdoor Classroom, the PORCH_house prefab project in Little Rock, Arkansas was designed to push the design–build model into the realm of contingent pedagogy. Conceived from the beginning as a multi-semester project,

FIGURE 4.1.4   PORCH_house prefab. Little Rock, AR, 2009–2010.

the BArch curriculum was adjusted to enable a core group of seven fifth-year students to participate from the beginning of the design phase through project delivery. While they were not exposed to the entire project acquisition phase or the contract negotiations, they were involved to some degree and once the design phase began they were engaged in all aspects of the project. As a result, the students were full collaborators who played a key role in navigating the myriad of dependent conditions encountered during the production of architecture. In addition, five fourth-year students were included in an attempt to capture and communicate knowledge from one year, and one project, to the next. These fourth-year students were also able to be involved with project acquisition, negotiations, and logistics for the next project.

The level of complexity engaged by the students was significant as the project involved a non-profit community developer, the homebuyer, a low-income mortgage provider, the mayor's office, a contractor of record who provided the legal structure for building inspections, two different municipal code enforcement agencies, and a diverse group of community organizations invested in the specific neighborhood. For this project the city where the prefabrication occurred was 200 miles from the city where the units were installed and each city had its own codes governing zoning, building, and inspections.

In the end, students developed a whole new set of skills involving adaptation, negotiation, and mental dexterity. Schedules were not always met, logistical challenges interrupted carefully designed timelines, and innumerable, unforeseen complications related to cost, contracts, and material availability conspired to compromise the idealized scenario, as is so often the case in reality.

Case study 04: American University of Sharjah Fabrication Initiative

As a relatively young institution the American University of Sharjah represents a *tabula rasa* opportunity to experiment with the development of alternative pedagogies based on immersive methods. The program benefits from extraordinary digital and analog fabrication equipment combined with a faculty majority committed to full-scale education and a department head familiar with the logistic and political hurdles. However, this recently acquired wealth of resources exists within a cultural context that doesn't celebrate the act of making.

FIGURE 4.1.5 The Thinker's Chair. Sharjah, UAE, 2012. Designer: Maha Habib.

FIGURE 4.1.6 Display wall rendering and AUS Digital Fabrication Lab.

A significant portion, if not a majority of students at the American University of Sharjah belong to this cosmopolitan context, and grew up in the UAE as foreign nationals. While they typically maintain close contact with their countries of origin, these students' life experiences have been formed within the context of the UAE. Often, there has been a similar rupture between this generation and their forbearers' material traditions – a rupture caused by dislocation rather than by development.

(Sarnecky 2012)

Over the past six years Prof. Bill Sarnecky has worked to introduce students to a culture of making through a series of furniture design–build courses. As student interest and capacity has increased a nascent tradition of making is beginning to emerge within the school. Larger and more complex projects, such as the display wall/seating, are now being engaged.

At the same time the faculty and facilities are being expanded to accommodate large investments in new analog and digital fabrication equipment. New faculty with a range of interests in a broadly defined realm of "fabrication" have been hired and, combined with existing faculty, the school benefits from a lineup of nine colleagues engaged in pedagogies of making.

Support for these ongoing efforts faces operational and logistical challenges posed by conflict between non-normative teaching methods and normative accreditation requirements. Moving forward, the program is committed to solving these challenges. Experiments with alternative teaching loads, team teaching, vertical studios, and a curriculum identified by an iterative, multi-stepped engagement with contingency are some of the items under discussion.

Note

1 Newbern Town Hall/Auburn University Rural Studio, 16 July 2013. Available online at: http://www.archdaily.com/400565/newbern-town-hall-auburn-rural-studio/ Accessed January 2014.

Reference

Sarnecky, William (2012). 'Building a Material Culture in Dubai'. *Journal of Architectural Education* 65(2): 80–88.

4.2

ARCHITECTURAL DELIBERATION

The Hyalite Pavilion

Bruce Wrightsman

Introduction

Hyalite Pavilion, a multi-use pavilion completed by the School of Architecture at Montana State University, offers an inventive construction-based Live Project template. Its unique design challenges required the abandonment of the normative requirement to complete a project within a semester or academic year time frame. In contrast, the completion of Hyalite Pavilion was a process of slow and careful movement learned through understanding and embracing the inherent challenges of the remote and harsh landscape. The result was an architecturally rewarding project which reconsidered traditional US Forest Service models to address the design realities of a remote mountain context.

The Forest Service and its architecture

> ... the interest of the visitor ... should concentrate on features of natural, in preference to artificial, beauty ... Architectural features should be confessedly subservient ...
>
> *Fredrick Law Olmstead*

The intent of architecture to fit harmoniously within a national forest context has its roots in the founding of the United States Forest Service. The agency's successful history includes many beautifully handcrafted and sensitively designed rustic structures of the Civilian Conservation Corps era that are still admired today.

The ongoing facility design goals of the US Forest Service are documented in the Building Environmental Image Guidelines (BEIG), which are used by all districts of the Forest Service. The agency's aspiration is to ensure thoughtful design and management of the built environment and to promote the principles of sustainability. These goals are consistent with the agency's role as a leader in land stewardship. In his commentary on the Old Faithful Inn at Yellowstone National park, Harvey Kaiser characterizes the three foundational principles of rustic design: the "use of natural, local materials, allusions to pioneer building techniques, and strong ties to the site" (United States Department of Agriculture 2001, Ch. 4.6). Current US Forest Service design should aspire to synthesize rustic style precedents with contemporary realities and needs.

Project structure

Hyalite Pavilion is located along the Hyalite Reservoir in the Gallatin National Forest, just south of Bozeman, Montana. The new pavilion serves a vital public need for covered recreational and social activities at a key spot within a popular day-use area.

The initial desire for the pavilion and the partnership with Montana State University came from Jane Ruchman, a US Forest Service landscape architect and recreation program manager. The design goal was to reinforce the positive image of the Forest Service as good stewards and conservationists by making sustainable choices in the built environment. Moreover, the goal was to make visiting Hyalite Pavilion an enlightening experience – one that helps people understand the forces of ecology and the nature of the forest landscape through the architecture.

The pavilion began as a directed research project that critically investigated the physical and environmental aspects of the day-use site. The goal of the research was to provide foundational information on the site, its context, and its value assessment for future design work. The analysis included physical, environmental, and experiential aspects of the site and immediate reservoir area as well as investigations of

FIGURE 4.2.1 Nested in an elevated mountainous region, the building site is located near an accessible hiking path along Hyalite Reservoir.

FIGURE 4.2.2 A detailed program analysis generated a series of winter and summer activities to be accommodated at the pavilion.

FIGURE 4.2.3 The pavilion is situated at the back of the site near a small inlet and built on a stone pedestal above grade. A tall stone fireplace anchors the entrance side. The compound sloping roofline is influenced by ridgelines of the surrounding mountain range.

current activities and uses at the reservoir area, a projection of how these activities would be impacted, and predictions of potential new activities.

The design phase began in the spring semester of 2009. The collaborative partnership between Montana State University, its School of Architecture, and

FIGURE 4.2.4 A masonry contractor worked on-site with design students teaching them the craft of laying masonry.

the Gallatin National Forest expanded to include business partnerships with a local structural engineer and a stone masonry company in Big Fork, Montana, which sponsored the iterative design process. Each of five initial students developed a building design strategy that incorporated stone masonry as a primary material. Through a series of design charrettes, two primary strategies emerged and were presented to the Gallatin National Forest. The final hybrid design solution best addressed the issues of site, material appropriateness, flexibility of use, and wheelchair accessibility.

The collaborative progression extended beyond the classroom. As part of the design process, students were actively engaged with a number of specialists, including structural and geotechnical engineers, materials consultants, and US Forest Service engineers and rangers. The project included 27 graduate and undergraduate students working with 5 community partners. The project budget of $43,000 was funded through a grant from the Gallatin National Forest Service.

Remoteness

> Opportunity is often missed because it's dressed in overalls and looks a lot like work.
>
> *Thomas Edison*

The site's region receives significant winter precipitation resulting in heavy snow load structural requirements. For the pavilion, this necessitated a robust roof

Hyalite Pavilion: Iterative schedule of experiments

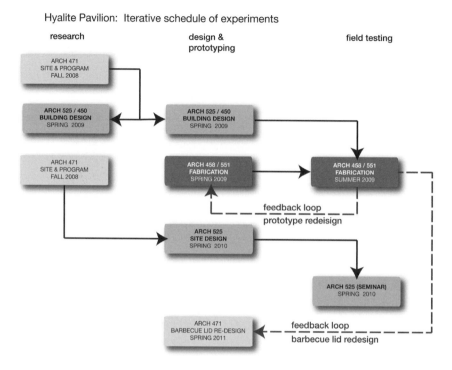

FIGURE 4.2.5   Hyalite Pavilion schedule.

structure. The long winters, however, coupled with the remoteness of the site, significantly limited the construction time available to build. Therefore, a hybrid solution of off-site prefabrication and site-built strategies was developed. This required a unique research and teaching strategy calibrated to the challenges of completing the work. The planning, design, and construction of the pavilion spanned six semesters.

The project was organized into a series of iterative experiments beginning with a research phase to develop a design strategy. Subsequent steps included creating a concept, fabricating prototypes of the prefabricated components, and testing on site before the project was redesigned for final construction. The prototyping was a mutable activity serving as a feedback loop, supporting the deliberation and imaginative engagement vital to the class learning objectives. Assessing the multiple transmutations required extending project development. Creating a detail or making a component had to be critically explored before it could be replicated multiple times at a high level of craftsmanship. The design and prototype testing were done on campus in a controlled shop environment prior to final installation. This allowed the project schedule to be more malleable, operating during times when on-site construction was severely limited. The challenges encountered during all phases inspired students and faculty to successfully create an inventive Live Project.

Hyalite Pavilion is unique compared with other US Forest Service projects. Its strategy challenged traditional design approaches, yet remained consistent with the US Forest Service's role as land steward and extended the architectural potential in highly sensitive national forest contexts.

Reference

United States Department of Agriculture (2001). *Building Environmental Image Guide for the National Forests and Grassland.* United States Department of Agriculture, Forest Service. FS-710.

4.3

PROVIDING PRACTICAL EXPERIENCE TOWARDS REGISTRATION AS AN ARCHITECT WITHIN THE CONTEXT OF A SUPPORTIVE ACADEMIC ENVIRONMENT

Live Projects as dual qualifications

Anne Markey

Introduction

The Sir John Cass Faculty of Art, Architecture and Design (The Cass) at London Metropolitan University places socially engaged practice at the core of its teaching. In support of this approach, it registered a Projects Office with the Royal Institute of British Architects in 2004 to bridge academic discourse and architectural practice. In 2012, with the creation of the Schools of Art, Architecture and Design, it was renamed Cass Projects.

The Projects Office operates at different scales – at the 1:1 of talking to others, making, drawing, and writing; at the mid-scale of built works, particularly with local communities in areas of deprivation; and at the larger national and international scale of educational and infrastructural project realization. It is directed by Professor Robert Mull, Dean of the Faculty, and Anne Markey, Director of Cass Projects, both experienced and practising architects. Two full-time architectural assistants, both Cass graduates, are employed permanently and part-time staff and students contribute on a project-by-project basis. Cass Projects increasingly assists students and graduates to obtain the practical experience necessary for architectural registration.

Architectural education in the UK is divided into three distinct parts: Part 1 typically comprises a three-year undergraduate degree followed by a year out in practice; Part 2 typically comprises a two-year postgraduate qualification; and Part 3 involves a further year in practice followed by a professional practice examination. The projects by Cass graduates highlighted here were also eligible for Part 1 and Part 3 practical experience. They include school projects in London, India, and Sierra Leone and infrastructure projects in India, Bosnia, and Sri Lanka. The projects allowed students and graduates to communicate directly with clients, users, and communities; navigate legislative, planning, and health and safety procedures; and complete programming, procurement, and construction. The projects, some external and some self-initiated, range from conventional commissions to pro bono community projects to design–build. All work produced by the Projects Office is covered by the University's Professional Indemnity Insurance.

London schools projects

Cass Projects has helped students and graduates over the years to execute a number of inner-city school projects in London's more deprived boroughs.

At Millfields School in Hackney the parents' association commissioned a master plan for their overcrowded playground on a land-locked inner-city site. We engaged the artist Martin Kaltwasser and students from the School of Architecture to involve schoolchildren in workshops to find out how they would like their playground to change. This resulted in a structure for imaginary play which also defines the junction between the junior and seniors areas. Jen Ng, a Part 3 student, is currently continuing work on a master plan to improve what is currently an unexciting tarmac expanse.

At Kingsmead Primary School in Hackney the Projects Office was invited to a limited competition on the basis of earlier work. We were appointed in Spring 2006 and the new classroom was completed for January 2007. During her Part 1 year out, London Met student Anna Page designed and oversaw the building of a new classroom for reception age children that included an outdoor learning area

FIGURE 4.3.1 Play structure for Millfields Primary School, Hackney with Martin Kaltwasser.

FIGURE 4.3.2 Classroom interior, Kingsmead School, Hackney.

FIGURE 4.3.3 Classroom, covered waiting area, and outdoor play area, Kingsmead School, Hackney.

and covered waiting area for parents. With a Part 2 student, Rashid Ali, she developed the detail drawings with the contractor firm, which had been selected for its fast-track building system and track record of working on innovative architectural designs.

The Aldgate Project and interdisciplinary projects

To mark the creation of the new Faculty of Art, Architecture and Design, the Projects Office invited academics to respond to the Aldgate Project in their teaching. More than 20 cross-disciplinary projects resulted during the academic year 2011–12, including participants from architecture, fine art, jewellery, furniture design, textiles design, and animation. Working with local community groups, charities, and stakeholders, tutors and students moved outside the confines of the studio space. One of the project's aims was to better connect the new faculty with its surrounding area in London's East End, a socially mixed, vibrant, but also complex inner-city area. Zoe Berman, a Part 3 student, received a follow-on commission from a local homelessness charity Providence Row to prepare a feasibility study exploring an urban garden's spatial potential to engage its homeless clients in meaningful occupation.

In 2012 John McDonnell MP invited The Cass to propose and establish public art and architecture projects in Hayes, Middlesex. In response, Cass Projects developed the Made in Hayes programme, a series of projects that will take place over the coming years. All projects will consider what great things have been, are being, and will be made there, and will generate ideas about how the town can continue to flourish. Jen Ng of Cass Projects wrote the Made in Hayes brief and is currently supporting funding applications to enable collaboration on a landscape improvement project. She will be able to use this work for her Part 3 practical experience.

International projects

Working on projects at a national level has helped us to undertake Live Projects internationally. In 2009 Bo Tang and Shamoon Patwari, two graduates, travelled to Sierra Leone, West Africa, with postgraduates to carry out a study of local building materials and construction techniques. This research will be published in an extensive volume. The study informed the development of a Live Project directed by Professor Maurice Mitchell for a new building for Ivor Leigh Memorial School, which opened in August 2011.

Tang and Patwari also completed a study on hygiene awareness in Kuchhpura, near Agra, India. Research gathered from local people influenced the design development for a low-cost sanitation system, implementing over 80 household septic tank toilets. The success of the toilet system, initially a prototype, has allowed Tang and Patwari to collaborate with the Indian NGO CURE on a decentralized wastewater treatment system to provide clean irrigation water for local farmers.

FIGURE 4.3.4 Ivor Leigh Memorial School, Sierra Leone, elevation, Bo Tang and Shamoon Patwari.

FIGURE 4.3.5 De-centralized wastewater treatment system at Kuchhpura, India.

There are plans to improve the area around the treatment system as a new public space. Their other projects in India include ten community classrooms for the children of quarry workers in Navi Mumbai in collaboration with the NGO ARPHEN.

Students have also carried out projects that emphasize their personal histories. One example is Vernes Causevic's 'Space for Exchange: A Sustainable Return to Srebrenica' (2010–11), which proposes a sustainable regional vocational education

FIGURE 4.3.6 Community classroom in Navi Mumbai, India.

centre. This project resulted in a commission through the Projects Office for Vernes to design a vocational education building in Bratunacin, Bosnia.

Another project currently supported by Cass Projects is Naveen Anandakumar's Kattankudy Water Management Scheme (2011–12). This commission was granted by a local community in Sri Lanka on which Naveen's research has focused. The project proposes a wastewater system that integrates with the existing physical and cultural infrastructure.

Cass Projects and professional registration

As Director, Anne Markey supervises all of Cass Projects' work and signs the documents students complete for licensure. The scale and funding demands of these commissions often mean that a longer period is needed to gain the experience required for UK architectural registration than in conventional practice. However, the need to prove understanding of law, practice, budget and fee management, and building procurement is difficult to achieve in any context within a one-year Part 3. Work at The Cass allows students to see projects through from start to finish. Cass Projects also encourages students to take an entrepreneurial approach to practice, initiating projects and funding them.

Conclusion

By enabling students to develop self-initiated projects and commissions, Cass Projects' supportive professional practice sends an important and positive message from the faculty. Conceived first and foremost to enable, the Projects Office quickly developed an agenda that mirrored the faculty's mission statement. Cass Projects quite simply asks that the projects it supports have a clear social purpose. Precisely this requirement has resulted in a portfolio of projects that engage the complex issues of health, education, and cultural heritage in areas subject to rapid change caused by poverty and political unrest.

Clients and users benefit from talented students and graduates who produce thoughtful responses to their particular situation and needs. The quality of the buildings produced by Cass students and graduates has been recognized by such programmes as the *Architects' Journal* Small Projects Award. Finally, the Projects Office works closely with the faculty's academics to ensure cross-fertilization between studio and office. Live Projects are used as a pedagogic tool and research method; design reviews and crits ensure project quality. Several Projects Office affiliates share academic duties. This combination of professional support and experience with an emphasis on a socially engaged architecture produces projects that are – regardless of their scale – ambitious in scope and intention.

4.4

sLAB (STUDENT LED ARCHITECTURE BUILD)

Developing the capability to develop meta-capabilities

Frank Mruk

Introduction

The New York Institute of Technology sLAB (Student Led Architecture Build) program evolved from individual projects that began to accrue. sLAB grew out of NYIT's successful 2005 and 2007 Solar Decathlon projects and NYIT's community design studio. sLAB projects are positioned as student-led design/build projects that are embedded in community. These projects are initially developed outside the curriculum by a committee of students and faculty. A problem is defined or selected and students self-organize into teams proposing solutions in a competition-based format. Professors are provided as coaches or, in some cases, co-collaborators. After a jury selects the best design, the project is introduced into the curriculum, where it is developed into a buildable solution. To make the project a reality, students actively participate in the fundraising, marketing, and building of the project. This case study demonstrates the introduction and adaptation of a competition-based student led design/build model and shows how these projects can introduce new dynamic meta-capabilities to the students and to the school.

Background

Models help organizations, teams, and humans receive information, process information, and respond accordingly. A conceptual model of how things work serves as a heuristic to help us navigate our environment. Meta-models are also very important. Students who are author/designers in a competition also gain the capacity to design the competition, raising them to a higher meta-plane which allows them to understand competitive strategy. Dynamic capability meta-models are a very important component of the NYIT program.

In 1997 David J. Teece, Gary Pisano, and Amy Shuen produced an important paper for the *Strategic Management Journal* titled "Dynamic Capabilities and Strategic Management" (Teece *et al.* 1997). They state that competitive advantage goes beyond the exploitation of existing internal and external capabilities by introducing the development of new capabilities. Dynamic Capabilities is based upon "the ability to integrate, build, and reconfigure internal and external competences to address rapidly changing environments" (Leonard-Barton 1992).

Case study: Solar Decathlon

The Green Machine | Blue Space 2005 Solar Decathlon strategy featured a unique hydrogen storage system rather than traditional batteries. The team joint ventured with the US Merchant Marine Academy to convert solar energy to hydrogen via a hydrogen fuel cell. The house was built and inaugurated as "America's First Solar Hydrogen Home" in 2007. The ribbon cutting ceremony at the US Merchant Marine Academy was preceded by a commencement address by President Bush. Under the direction of the NREL (National Renewable Energy Lab), the home was used as a research tool for developing Solar Hydrogen household systems. Soon after the competition the NYIT students were invited to testify about the benefits of solar technology to the US Congress.

OPEN House, NYIT's entry in the 2007 Solar Decathlon, was conceived as an open access and open source residence. In this evolving experiment, anyone anywhere has full access to the design and can modify it for any environment. The students encourage the downloading of their plans to "build your own OPEN House!" The plans and specifications were featured on the front page of Cameron Sinclair's "Open Architecture Network" (http://openarchitecturenetwork.org/node/1081 Accessed January 2014).

FIGURE 4.4.1 "America's First Solar Hydrogen House," Solar Decathlon, 2005.

FIGURE 4.4.2   Solar Decathlon, 2007.

Case study: PAL Boxing

Students met Joe Higgins, Director of PAL Boxing in Freeport, NY, while doing research for another design studio. Joe had taken several disadvantaged youths and converted them into Olympic boxing contenders. Working in teams of three, the students self-organized to develop designs for a new boxing gym and held a competition to decide the winning scheme. The two finalist submissions were combined and developed in a design development studio. The team presented their solutions to the Mayor of Freeport at a town council meeting, which was open to the public and televised.

Case study: Hostos Dream Project

Students traveled to the Dominican Republic to do research for an innovative new school called the Hostos Dream Project. The students developed plans for a modular school made from shipping containers (the first in the Dominican Republic). The student team spent three days in Higuey visiting existing schools and promoting the project through local talk shows and press conferences. The project was well received by the public and the local government, who have long awaited an improvement in the schools in their underserved communities.

An innovative new thatched roofing system made out of up-cycled water bottles was invented for this project. The bottles are cut on a template and screwed together to form a tile-like roofing system. The system requires a customized connector into which the bottles are screwed. These connectors serve as the pallet for delivering the water bottles. A provisional patent for the system was issued and the project won a jurors' choice award at the prestigious New York State Business Plan Competition.

FIGURE 4.4.3 Soda Bib Project.

Case study: Nosara Recycling Center

NYIT architecture students worked on a competition to develop a recycling and education center in Costa Rica. The project involved the community service chapters of Freedom by Design and Engineers without Borders. Veritas University in San Jose, Costa Rica, served as the local partner for the project. The project implemented two fundraising campaigns on Kickstarter.com that raised over $30,000. The students involved are currently working with film director Ayana de Vos on a film about the project and their work was recently exhibited in the Museum of Modern Art's 2013 show "Cut 'n' paste: From assemblage to collage city."

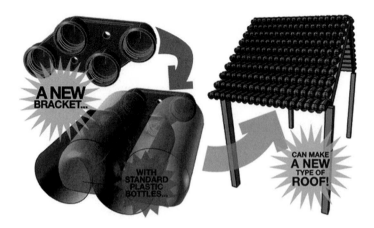

FIGURE 4.4.4 sLAB Nosara Recycling Center.

FIGURE 4.4.5   Comprehensive Coastal Communities competition.

Operation Resilient Long Island and the Comprehensive Coastal Communities Competition

Hurricane Sandy hit the New York Metropolitan area on October 29, 2012. The track of the storm, the resultant storm surge, and the devastation were all unprecedented. Within two weeks of the storm a group of students approached the NYIT sLAB committee, saying: "we need to find an effective way to help." Within days they had organized orLI (Operation Resilient Long Island). The students met with residents and community organizations on some of the hardest-hit sites, and with emergency management officials and local building department officials to assess the situation; they then produced a brochure for residents describing important issues in rebuilding. They initiated a rebuilding design charrette and organized a symposium where they brought together numerous groups from New York, New Jersey, and Long Island, including universities, government officials, and community groups, to discuss the different strategies being implemented in each region. One major result of all this activity was the student-led launch of the Comprehensive Coastal Communities (3C) competition, which crowd-sourced ideas for rebuilding from over 300 designers from around the world. Winners were announced at a student-organized TEDx (http://www.youtube.com/watch?v=8HbaGcqgxD4 Accessed January 2014) event.

Conclusion

All of the above projects have brought numerous new capabilities into the school and into the students' repertoires. These include the ability to self-organize, the ability to effectively manage interdisciplinary teams, the ability to obtain a patent, the ability to construct architecture, the ability to fundraise and market, the ability to participate in a documentary film, and the ability to reframe a problem and convey a solution to community groups, mayors, and congressmen. The students have experienced firsthand the social entrepreneurship capabilities needed to start something, to get it off the ground, and to marshal a bold new initiative through to completion.

Most importantly, at NYIT, the application of these new capabilities has evolved a higher meta-plane. For example, the ability to effectively compete to develop solutions to a problem grew into the ability to crowd-source ideas which effectively allow people from around the world to compete to develop solutions to a problem. This new meta-level of attack was also apparent in the students' ability to reframe a competition on solar energy as an ability to produce hydrogen, to conceive a new school in the Dominican Republic as the opportunity for a new up-cycled roofing patent, or to see a new recycling center in Costa Rica as the site of a documentary film on the problems of waste removal which in turn fed building fundraising efforts on Kickstarter.com. In all these examples, the students fundamentally own the problem and organically shift paradigms in order to work on a more effective, higher meta-plane. This dynamic meta-capability (the capability to quickly transcend to a higher, more effective meta-platform) in response to unanticipated and previously unseen problems becomes in and of itself a capability much needed in rapid change environments.

References

Leonard-Barton, D. (1992). "Core Capabilities and Core Rigidities: A Paradox in Managing New Product Development." *Strategic Management Journal*, 13: 111–125.

Teece, D.J., Pisano, G., and Shuen, A. (1997). "Dynamic Capabilities and Strategic Management." *Strategic Management Journal*, 18: 509–533.

4.5

VOICES FROM NAGAPATTINAM

Revisiting communities after the 2004 tsunami

Sofia Davies

Introduction

This chapter considers how an interdisciplinary group of students utilised the Participatory Rapid Appraisal approach to broaden their own skills and expertise as well as redefine the role of the architect in response to communities' recovery from the Asian tsunami of 2004.

In January 2012 MA Development and Emergency Practice students – of which I was one – from Oxford Brookes University embarked on a Live Project in India. The cohort included a mix of architecture students and students studying subjects from Journalism to International Relations. For the architecture students specifically, the Masters Programme offered the opportunity for their studies to take an alternative structure in which they could spend some time out of the conventional design studio, learning principles and theories from the humanitarian sector. Joining the students from Oxford Brookes in India were architecture students from the University of Georgia.

These students were to carry out community engagement research in Tamil Nadu, south-east India in collaboration with the NGO Resource Centre for Participatory Development Studies (RCPDS) and rural communities in Nagapattinam, Tamil Nadu. The research focused on the response and recovery following the tsunami of December 2004 in the Indian Ocean. Nagapattinam was the worst affected region in India, accounting for 76 per cent of deaths in Tamil Nadu. Over 6,000 people lost their lives and approximately 40,000 houses were destroyed (Kumaraperumal *et al.* 2007).

The project would see students put theory into practice as they took the lead in engaging with the community and carrying out the research. Given Terms of Reference (TOR), the students then used their studies and theories to inform the structure of the community engagement. Following the extraction of information,

FIGURE 4.5.1 The reconstruction of Vizuntha Mavadi: a map drawn by members of the community illustrating the location of post-tsunami housing within the village.

recommendations were made to government officials and other NGOs, resulting in a published report.

The Live Project

The objective was to formulate six recommendations in accordance with the TOR.

The main research method used was Participatory Rapid Appraisal (PRA). Tools included semi-structured interviews with community members, physical mapping, transect walks, timelines of events, seasonal calendars, daily activity schedules, venn diagrams, and matrix ranking. After completion of the PRA tools, the findings were presented back to the villagers to ensure that the interpretation was accurate.

The recommendations were confirmed as priority actions by the communities visited, Gramathu Medu and Vizuntha Mavadi, and endorsed by local NGOs and government officials.

The Live Project then formed the basis of the design studio, with students producing individual projects based upon solutions addressing the findings in the report.

Lessons learnt

Preparation is key

Location or context is an integral part of any design scheme. In this case, the humanitarian issues were originally taught and discussed in a lecture theatre in the UK, far removed from where those issues are actually located. Therefore, thorough

FIGURE 4.5.2 Maintaining cultural sensitivity: a group, predominantly of women from the village, are given the opportunity to have a voice, without judgement from large groups of men from the village.

preparation was vital. This project taught the students that cultural nuances and social and official structures are fundamental in understanding the context in which theory will be applied. Preparation in learning and understanding these factors allows for mutual respect in the field and a more relaxed form of rapport building, which, in turn, may be more fruitful in extracting useful information.

Preparing mentally to 'learn on the job' is key, as it presents its own challenges in terms of cultural and social sensitivity. Conventional education methods may not prepare students adequately, but a Live Project offers the opportunity to understand the practicalities and realities of practice, making one aware of the highs and lows that may be experienced and the responsibilities and boundaries that must be worked within when in the field.

The ability to adapt

Just as preparation is key, the ability to adapt is vital to the success of any engagement with the community. It was evident that, working in two different communities for this project, a 'one size fits all' approach was not appropriate. Each community is different and therefore the students learnt that adapting methods and plans for each was essential.

Before embarking on the project each group selected the tools needed according to the TOR for that group. Many of the tools had to be adapted or used in conjunction with semi-structured interviews. In addition, it became clear during the process that some voices within the community were louder

FIGURE 4.5.3   Using the architects' PRA tools the fishermen illustrate the size of their catch for each month of the year.

than others and some conflicted with each other, depending on people's personal experiences. The student-led nature of the project meant that the students' observation skills were paramount in identifying these issues and reacting accordingly.

In relation to the physical architecture of the villages, cyclone-proof houses were built for the communities. These were meant to be inexpensive and quick to built. During the Live Project it transpired that these houses did not take into account cultural complexities such as social hierarchy or gender issues, environmental factors, maintenance and opportunities for extensions, or infrastructure, including public transport and connections to other villages. In the ideal world of a design studio time is spent dissecting and analysing a brief, and maintaining the design's appropriateness to its context. In reality these aspects may be neglected owing to constraints of timescale and budget. Many of the aspiring architects on this trip were inspired to design alternatives that took a holistic and participative approach to design, with the idea of empowering communities to develop their own creativity and influence the shape of their lives.

FIGURE 4.5.4 A mix of students from Oxford Brookes and the University of Georgia work together in utilising their skills appropriately, giving a voice to more members of the community to understand further the varied needs, fears and ambitions.

Working with other professionals

This particular Live Project showed how collaboration between architects and other professionals can be a positive experience. Firstly, it reflects the work place, where architects must work with other consultants in order to deliver a project.

Secondly, working alongside the other Masters students, who came from various professional backgrounds, allowed for the range of knowledge and experience to influence that of the architecture students. The Live Project indicated that, while aid can be mainly resource driven and focused on the physical, the PRA tools used allowed all practitioners to investigate the social aspects and soft assets of a community, gaining a deeper understanding of its priorities and needs. The project went on to influence the direction of the design studio heavily; as a result the architecture students broadened their scope, thinking beyond the built environment, addressing social, economical, and political structures and concepts through design.

Ultimately, theory can be limiting; therefore, Live Projects are essential in building knowledge and preparing for the work place. They also build students' confidence in their capabilities. While one Live Project is not enough to create an expert, multiple Live Projects would provide the opportunity to learn from previous experiences and mistakes and embed the knowledge and practice further. This can lead to improved competency in the work place.

Additionally, the project's student leadership allowed for self-appraisal, the chance to converse with peers, and the opportunity to learn to compromise, adapt, and think laterally and innovatively.

FIGURE 4.5.5 Designing conversations. Simply talking to community members is a skill these students have learnt is a necessity in forming relationships with the communities they are working with to produce a more meaningful outcome.

Architects: their role, skills, and expertise

This Indian Live Project certainly 'opened the eyes' of the architecture students and allowed them to realise alternative roles for the architect as an enabler and a facilitator who empowers others. Through their participation, communities are given a voice in which an architect's conventional role changes from that of the informer to the informed. An architect's alternative role is to facilitate a design or process instigated primarily by the community themselves, resulting in a sense of ownership and therefore greater sustainability.

Our skills as architects go far beyond designing a building. While in the field, the project indulged the students' creativity in design conversations that gave a voice to the community, enabling them to reach empowered decisions that altered their lives. Back in the studio, the Live Project influenced the design studio to a great degree. Using their skills as problem solvers, the architecture students continued to take the lead in addressing the problems that had emerged from the trip. They found themselves designing not a physical structure but a process allowing for education and the development of skills, playing an integral part in improving the livelihoods of the communities visited. Designing in this way can result in building a community's resilience to potential shocks and stresses.

This Live Project and the use of PRA had a great influence on the direction of the design studio back at the university. Without this experience, the students' projects would have extended to nothing more than well-meaning speculation.

Reference

Kumaraperumal, R., Natarajan, S., Sivasamy, R., Chellamuthu, S., Ganesh, S., and Anandakumar, G. (2007). 'Impact of Tsunami 2004 in Coastal Villages of Nagapattinam District, India'. *Science of Tsunami Hazards: The International Journal of the Tsunami Society*, 26(2): 93–114.

4.6

THE FARESHARE LIVE PROJECT

Simon Warren

This prefabricated interior office space project, installed within a warehouse used for local food redistribution, challenged student ingenuity to design, source, and build all components within a minimal budget and timeframe.

In *Spatial Agency*, Awan, Schneider, and Till critique established forms of architectural education as 'the continuation of the master tutor and willing servant students, the privileging of the visual, the inculcation of absurd modes of behaviour (sleep deprivation, aggressive defensiveness, internal competition), the raising of individuals onto pedestals' (Awan *et al.* 2011: 37–46). This description provides a compelling argument for the role of Live Projects in architectural pedagogy and their potential for a broad range of outcomes as an antidote to the limitations of the traditional design studio. Live Projects could be seen as 'complementary' and in the very best hands 'alternative' to orthodox design studio work (Rural Studio's remarkable work in Alabama (Rural Studio 2014) being an appropriate example).

Collaborative endeavour

The point of departure of the Live Project is that collaboration and collective endeavour are at the heart of pedagogic purpose. The project for FareShare (FareShare 2014), a national charity that addresses food poverty and food waste, commenced with two design workshops for participating students.

By suppressing individual competition and encouraging collaboration, the students were set to work in groups of four, focusing on two themes: the development of the brief and their assessment of the design constraints. Providing input to the groups through face to face conversations were key people from FareShare, and also the structural engineer and project manager. This was the first time that students were designing for someone other than themselves; this model of work promoted team working, with the participation of the client, professionals, and

FIGURE 4.6.1   Students presenting initial ideas at the first design workshop.

students as equals. Students soon perceived their value in the collaborative process and appreciated that the professionals were taking them seriously. This showed that exposing architecture students to an appropriate 'real world' context, particularly at undergraduate level, can develop understanding, maturity, and professionalism.

Towards the end of the first workshop the student teams presented their initial thoughts coherently and with confidence. There was consensus on the location of the office structure within the warehouse and on the use of timber for its construction, and there was agreement on the room sizes. Students appeared not to judge but to support each other and an unexpected outcome was that the forum seemed to empower normally less vocal students to contribute effectively. Over the course of the project the group dynamic illustrated that students who were not considered the best in a design-studio context were in fact very good organisers and strategists, and a few were talented in the creative use and detailing of materials.

The second design workshop, conducted in the same format a few days later, resulted in a sketch design.

Eureka!

The next challenge was to prepare for construction, developing the design and completing working drawings within a £1,500 budget. The decision to construct with timber was straightforward, but how could this be achieved within such a restriction? Students considered a number of construction proposals by sketching details, specifying materials, and checking costs. All propositions were assessed and judged to be over budget.

At this point the team witnessed a 'eureka' moment when one student suggested a different approach: the group should firstly source cheap and available materials and then design the structure. A number of students fired up their laptops and, after many items had been rejected, an eBay purchase of 200 sheets of plywood offcuts 450mm by 2400mm and 4mm thick determined the design solution. One over-keen student volunteered to stay up until 1 a.m. to make sure that the group were able to win the auction, with a bid of £46.05.

By this act students had rethought the design process from design-driven to resource-driven. In doing so they perceived something important and liberating: that there are ways of designing buildings that are different from the design-studio experience.

Economics and pedagogy

Normally design-studio processes do not have financial implications other than a cursory visitation once in a while. The pedagogical benefit of economics is seen as minor or distracting from the purpose of pure architecture. Notwithstanding this, budget is a real design constraint, just like site and gravity, and it needs a critical examination in schools of architecture. The introduction of economic constraints in a design environment has proved more effective than the discussion of budget considerations in lecture settings. This is where a Live Project has the edge over the orthodox design-studio project: the budget is a real rather than an artificial consideration.

Construction and pedagogy

A comprehensive design quickly emerged once the key plywood component was established. The group then devised the representation of fabrication and assembly requirements by replicating the method of product instruction manuals (IKEA being the most familiar) so that they could determine step by step how the building would be erected on site. This included tool schedules and a comprehensive list of material quantities, down to the number of nails and screws.

Construction took place over ten weeks during summer. We had underestimated how long it would take to complete; however, we had a supportive client who did not have a strict deadline, so this did not become a problem. The message is: when undertaking a Live Project, allow plenty of contingency time.

During the project we observed that 'time' has a pedagogical impact, as when students planned out a time-efficient construction through division of labour and prefabrication processes. Students recognised that time mattered in architectural production, as it potentially affected the aesthetic of the project.

Initially 42 450mm × 2400mm wall panels were pre-fabricated. The building footprint was then set out on the warehouse floor and the structural softwood

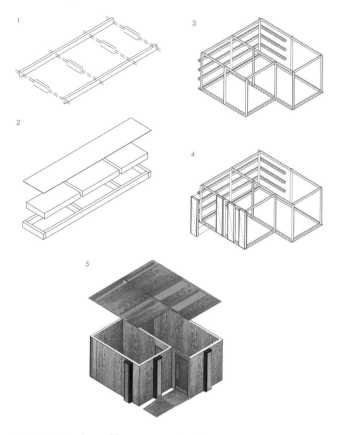

FIGURE 4.6.2 Assembly sequence drawing.

frame erected. The wall panels were screw fixed to the frame. Flooring, glazing, roof, electrical installation, and decoration followed.

Students commented on the significance of spending an appropriate amount of time working through the construction drawing sequence. Architecture is a unique art in that its production, unlike that of the artist, is carried out by a third party, the information being communicated through an intermediate process of construction drawings, specifications, and schedules. By having to build the project themselves students were able to make this connection firsthand. Undergraduate architecture students may never have the opportunity to visit a working building site during their studies, and these experiences allowed them to develop some appreciation of the complexity of building construction.

Time factors

For educators one difficulty in setting up Live Projects is the issue of time, particularly their co-ordination with the academic calendar. We believe that the successful

FIGURE 4.6.3 Panel fabrication.

FIGURE 4.6.4 Structural frame construction.

FIGURE 4.6.5 Pre-fab panels fixed to structural frame.

FIGURE 4.6.6 The FareShare Live Project completed.

delivery of a Live Project programme relies on flexibility rather than on its positioning in a specific area of the course because of the 'time' dynamic and the capacity to thematically or pedagogically complement other learning activities. At the Leeds School of Architecture Live Projects are delivered in the design studio (either as short intensive design charrettes or as longer semester projects), in technology modules, or in discrete university-wide events. The mapping of the project contents against the ARB/EU criteria for architectural education is both necessary and, in our experience, remarkably straightforward (an indication of the rich outcomes of Live Projects per se).

The FareShare project was extra-curricular. In a 'credit chasing' culture, participating students discovered that it can be empowering to do something because one wants to, and realised that they can be the masters of their education and experience.

Virtually all Live Projects are 'live' for a lot longer than the space one can create within the academic framework for their realisation. From the outset the need of the support of a 'project office', an architectural consultancy within the university, was recognised. A 'project office' within the School of Architecture enables academic staff to keep projects running outside the semester teaching structure; it also administers projects when they do not have an obvious or straightforward pedagogical impact.

Force for good

As Awan, Schneider, and Till reflect, 'If you ask a potential architecture student why they want to study architecture, the most common response is along the lines of "I want to design buildings and make the world a better place"' (Awan *et al.* 2011: 37–46). For most, the world is a precarious place and now more than ever architects are well placed to make a difference to people's lives.

The overarching pedagogical value of Live Projects is their potential impact as a force for good. They equip students to make informed choices about the kind of architect they would like to be, particularly in raising the issues of social responsibility. They offer meaningful contributions to our communities and built environment. The resource we have in abundance in architecture schools is our students, and they can be activated as a force for good. Besides their direct pedagogical role, Live Projects could produce a beneficial legacy in the wider community.

Acknowledgements

Client:	FareShare (West Yorkshire)
Funding organisations:	Land Securities, Batley Roundtable, Leeds Metropolitan University
Donations:	Various individuals via Freegle, Bradford Community RePaint

Consultants:	Buro Four – John Murphy, Buro Happold – Sarah Cropley
Students:	Rachael Branton, Claire Burrell, Zoltan Deak, Alex Durie, Antonia Frondella, Ron Graham, Harry Hewlett, Jamie Ho, Nick Jones, Aimee Major, Vahagn Mkrtchyan, Tom Partridge
Friends:	Phil Taylor, Chris Needham, Vikram Kaushal

References

Awan, N., Schneider, T., and Till, J. (2011). *Spatial Agency. Other Ways of Doing Architecture.* Routledge.

FareShare (2014). Available online at: liveprojectsnetwork.org/project/fareshare-project/ Accessed January 2014.

Rural Studio (2014). Available online at: http://www.ruralstudio.org/ Accessed January 2014.

4.7

BUILDING PROCESS

The Oxford Academy Live Project

Charlie Fisher and Natasha Lofthouse

Introduction

During our time as architecture students at Oxford Brookes University we participated in a three-year Live Project with Oxford Academy, a state school for 11–18-year-olds. Beginning with a short Live Project in collaboration with Oxford City Council, we designed a series of interventions for the school and gained skills ranging from capacity building to fundraising and construction, which led to numerous opportunities after graduation. This chapter highlights the processes we experienced while working with both the client, Oxford City Council, and the school during the ongoing live studio project. By undertaking an investigation into skills, relationships, tools, and competencies, inside and outside the studio, we speculate that there needs to be a change in the way that briefs are written.

Architectural practices frequently complain that graduates are not adequately prepared for industry. While we believe that the cultivation of creativity is vital for students, this needs to be combined with real projects at an early stage to prepare for the realities of working in practice. With reference to our own experiences, we suggest that one of the primary causes of this lack of student preparation for the real world lies within written studio briefs and emphasis given to problem solving within fictional narratives in schools of architecture today.

Leading the Live Project and co-authoring the brief

The original brief comprised three requirements: (1) a feature to mark the school entrance, (2) a facade system to cover an old building, and (3) a 'trim trail' that linked the sports hall to the playing fields. After discussing the three areas of the brief we went on a site visit with our client from Oxford City Council. After seeing the three sites and consulting with specialists we quickly realised that some elements of the brief were inappropriate owing to limited funds and health and

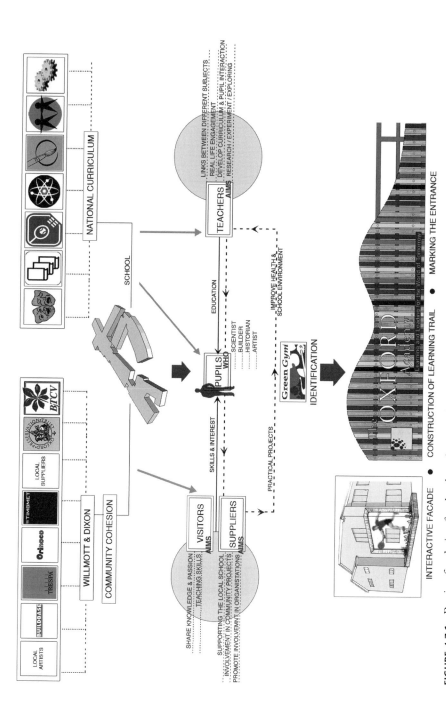

FIGURE 4.7.1 Recipe for design for the three interventions.

safety restrictions. One of the biggest obstacles was the masking of the unappealing technology 'k-block' building with a new facade system. The expectations were too great, however, given the time scale and lack of funding available to us for materials. During the process of designing the trim trail and facade system we realised that we needed to rewrite the brief to produce a more suitable set of design outcomes that would work within the evident time and budget constraints.

Given the unpredictable nature of real-life construction projects, we felt that we benefited from our tutors' encouragment to modify and even rigorously question the appropriateness of the brief. We argue that, were this option was more widely available within design-studio teaching, students would be better able to expand their skill-set as fully as possible.

The brief required us to represent the identity of the Academy and highlight the school's specialisations. These prerequisites led us in creating designs for the entrance and facade system, but, most importantly, they drove the process behind the design of the new learning trail. We wanted to involve the pupils via the school's own construction course, aware that this would 'cultivate ownership and, with it, a sense of belonging and responsibility' (Hamdi 2010). We felt that by handing over creative power to the pupils and teachers we would help initiate an ongoing programme of self-built interventions that might span a number of years. Regrettably, however, this was not deemed possible by the school.

Leading the project

After the initial two-week design period we presented our ideas to our tutors, studio peers, and clients from Oxford City Council. Although some of the design aspects were criticised owing to their limited aesthetic ambition, which was attributable to the lack of available materials, we received praise for the levels of rigour in the detailing and the overall management of the project.

Leading the project: beyond the academic timeframe

Although we finished the design studio that had set up the Live Projects in May 2011, we were encouraged to keep running the Oxford Academy Live Project. Given how much we felt we were learning and what it would mean in terms of gaining practical experience that would count towards our final qualification, we were keen to do so. In July 2011 we developed our designs in response to the comments made during our studio review and presented them to the headteacher, financial director, and design team of the new Academy.

The school gave the go-ahead to the outdoor learning trail as it tied in with the proposed plans for the adjacent wetlands area. A meeting was set up with the school's alternative curriculum team to discuss opportunities for integrating the project into the Academy's curriculum. We considered how the project might contribute to the course programme and what the students were capable of doing practically. Funding was essential for taking the project forward so we applied to

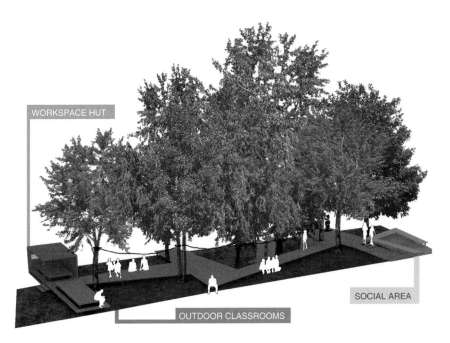

FIGURE 4.7.2 Proposed boardwalk and shelter.

FIGURE 4.7.3 Proposed outdoor classroom area.

FIGURE 4.7.4 Meeting with the Oxford Academy finance director.

FIGURE 4.7.5 Presentation to Oxford Brookes Community Fund donors.

the Oxford Brookes Alumni Association and the Santander Student Fund and raised £4,500. We also secured material sponsorship from Timbmet, a local timberyard, and Ecosheet, a recycled sheet-plastics company. We agreed to compile a set of construction documents for the project to be integrated into the Academy 2013/14 academic year. This was presented in an IKEA-style construction package, along with the donated and bought materials, to enable students and teachers to easily assemble the design and use the same construction process for any further projects.

Design studio versus Live Projects

In a typical design studio it is often difficult to understand the limits that time and budget constraints can create, yet these were of critical importance throughout our Live Project. When the studio project had finished and we were working on a one-to-one basis with the school outside the studio environment, new problems arose. For example, we learned that alterations and developments to the brief can occur at

FIGURE 4.7.6 Prototype construction model for the learning trail shelter.

various stages throughout the design process: after site and client meetings, during the conceptual and development stage, or during the build itself. We had to accept changes and respond with a professional attitude at all times, regardless of the point at which these alterations were made.

Unanticipated outcomes from the Oxford Academy project

As a result of this project we have created strong networks between the school, university, and neighbouring communities. The project taught us vital communication and people skills as well as time and budget management. It also opened up numerous opportunities for us during our time at Oxford Brookes and subsequently, in our professional careers.

In discussion with students involved in other Live Projects within our school of architecture, we agreed that we learned about communication, output, product, client and user interaction, brief making, materiality, and finance – issues that are not usually covered in design studio. For this reason, we feel that design studios should engage with everyday scenarios that are dealt with in practice: real people, along with social, political, and environmental obstacles. Good communication and good working relationships between all involved are key to these fast-paced projects having successful learning outcomes. The Oxford Academy project engaged with these elements and taught us a new way of working.

Concluding insight

The objective of a Live Project should not be to meet the requirements set in the brief. Instead, it concerns the ripples that the exercise creates – a legacy within the community we worked with. Both the school pupils and the architecture students benefited from collaborating and gaining new skills. The success of a Live Project is heavily reliant on the shared information flow between members of the project team and the implementation of a strong and adaptable brief to achieve a successful and rewarding experience for all. Getting students to work under these constraints to gain these skills is vital if they are to understand how to respond to difficulties and problems in communities outside their own.

Reference

Hamdi, N. (2010). *A Placemaker's Guide to Building Community*. Earthscan.

4.8

"IN THE PEOPLE'S INTEREST?"

Design/build Live Projects and public education

Christopher Livingston and Shauntel Nelson

Introduction

Written to combine the insights of professor and student, our chapter seeks to examine how design/build Live Project programs engage the fabric of university and college campuses and allow for a wide range of student participation, including active hands-on learning and passive observation. Furthermore, we contend that Live Projects enable a holistic enactment of the land-grant mission and nurture a greater appreciation for the built environment among participating students.

For almost a decade now, design/build Live Projects have been a valuable resource for instruction, creative activity, and service requirements at Montana State University (MSU). Executed by various faculty in an entrepreneurial spirit, Live Projects have engaged students and faculty in real-world issues and have been a benefit to both the local and global communities. These projects have been motivated principally by two conditions – although these certainly do not represent a definitive list – which we feel reflect the values of our institution and the profession at large. The first is the land-grant mission and the promise of the dissemination of knowledge to the broader community of the state and beyond. This mission is reflected not only in our work but also in MSU vision statements and, while not all institutions can claim land-grant origin, virtually all US institutions of higher learning have been impacted by the pervasiveness of the land-grant mission. Secondly, the presence of the Danforth Chapel on our campus provides a notable design/build precedent for our work. Designed and built by students and faculty, the Danforth Chapel demonstrates in its execution a spirit of university-wide collaboration and cooperation which is as progressive today as it was when the Chapel was completed in 1952.

The promise of the land-grant mission

The federal land-grant colleges, including Montana State University, were created under the Morrill Act of 1862, in which federal land was given to each respective state with the intent that the sale of these lands would be invested to create a 'perpetual fund' for each institution (Frye 1993: 40). With this funding, the resultant land-grant institutions would promote and carry out the education of the populace from all social classes in the practical methods of agriculture, science, and the mechanical arts. The rationale for the land-grant system was based on two basic beliefs. The first was the importance of education through the universities to create what Jonathan Baldwin Turner termed "thinking laborers" rather than "laborious thinkers" (ibid.: 41). Turner writes: "The most natural and effectual mental discipline possible for any man arises from setting him to earnest and constant thought about things he daily does, sees, and handles, and all their connected relations and interests" (Carriel 1911: 89). Turner's view was based on the idea that applied studies, as opposed to the pursuit of classical studies, would better prepare students for a career outside of the classroom. The second belief is that in a democracy all citizens should be allowed access to higher education, which would in turn create a more creative and prosperous society (Frye 1993: 41). Fundamentally, knowledge gained at the university would be directly applied to the real challenges faced by the citizenry of the state.

While differences exist from state to state and from institution to institution, the outcome of the land-grant mission – classical education incorporated with research and service and the ability to return knowledge to the general populace – would become a characteristic found almost universally in our system of higher education. Describing the pervasive character of the land-grant system, Johnson writes:

> In their original rebellion against classical instruction only, they put things scientific at the center, around which an unusually strong research orientation has developed, with an emphasis on application and problem solving. Thus was born the now famous academic trilogy: instruction, research, and service – a mission description that virtually every institution, public or private, now embraces, however different the interpretation.
>
> *(Johnson 1981: 334)*

We believe that the land-grant mission in its varied interpretations is uniquely suited to benefit from the design/build process. Opportunities for construction experience enhanced by material understanding and actual client interactions are only a few of the experiences that enhance traditional architectural training and prepare students for life beyond the classroom. Additionally, design/build projects located directly on university and college campuses, including the Danforth Chapel described below, provide not only practical experience for participating students but passive viewing for students not engaged in the process, allowing all students to gain a general understanding of the building process.

Precedent: the Danforth Chapel

The Danforth Chapel is a modest non-denominational chapel located at the heart of the Montana State University campus. Designed and built by students between

FIGURE 4.8.1 Danforth Chapel, Montana State University.

1949 and 1952 with a $5,000 grant from the Danforth Foundation, this project is a successful model in the design/build arena, primarily as a result of university-wide departmental collaboration in its construction, which included the schools of architecture, engineering, industrial arts, art, and horticulture, as well as support from the local community and the construction industry.

In his undergraduate thesis Milstein (1951) describes the breadth of collaboration and cooperation throughout the project. Milstein, a senior architecture student, developed the design of the chapel as his undergraduate thesis. Many of the architecture faculty assisted Milstein in this process, overseeing the design and later supervising the construction documents as well as performing construction supervision. Students and faculty from the School of Engineering also provided services on the project. The civil engineering faculty oversaw students in surveying the site, while a student in mechanical engineering designed, as his master's thesis, the radiant floor heating system. Additionally, students from the electrical engineering department designed both the electrical system and the lighting, and faculty from the industrial arts department supervised both architecture and industrial arts students in the concrete work as well as the carpentry, including both the framing and finish work. Students from the art department designed and built a stained glass window for the entry vestibule as well as all of the interior furnishings. Finally, in a lesser role, the horticulture department worked with students in the school of architecture to create a landscape plan for the grounds surrounding the chapel.

Towards the end of the construction phase, the project benefited from local fundraising and donated construction labor from townspeople and the local unions. So significant for its time was it that the Danforth design/build figured prominently

FIGURE 4.8.2 Danforth Chapel construction photo, 1951.

in an article published in *Architectural Record* on Montana State College, emphasizing new ideas within academic training and suggesting that design/build was a method "for closing the gap between school and office" (Anon. 1951). We see the completion of the Danforth Chapel as a highly visible model in design/build pedagogy primarily owing to the myriad performers, who included students and faculty from various departments, the university administration, and trade unions, as well as the local community.

Additionally, we feel that academic design/build opportunities may begin to expand the current cultural capital of the profession that Stevens (1998) describes beyond that of the intellectual and aesthetic to possibly begin to bridge the gap between our allied fields, including the construction industry. The recent repositioning efforts of the American Institute of Architects, emphasizing the architect's role as the "connective tissue between all players in the building industry" and as "the essential and strategic collaborator who leads the entire building process" (American Institute of Architects 2012), would seem to warrant such a move.

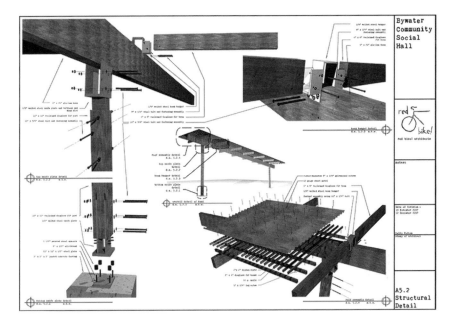

FIGURE 4.8.3 Construction documents, 2009. Student: Kelly Fulton.

FIGURE 4.8.4 Student material study – soy plastic, Spring 2006.

Conclusion

The land-grant mission has been largely subsumed into the fabric of higher education today. Architectural education, while not one of the disciplines originally addressed by the Morrill Act, is certainly aligned with the vestiges of this land-grant mission, as are the very tenets of the architectural profession. While the academy prepares students for the profession, we have questioned whether the current level of construction knowledge is sufficient in today's rapidly changing technological world. We believe that design/build has the ability to augment the current model of architectural education through projects which focus on areas including construction knowledge, thus enhancing material understanding and collaboration with our allied fields.

In these visible projects in an academic setting both active and passive learning is available to all students, all of which has the potential for creating knowledge that can be returned back to the community, wherever that may be in our increasingly globalized world.

References

American Institute of Architects (2012). *AIA Repositioning Summary: August 2012.* Available online at: http://www.aia.org/about/AIAB095945?dvid=&recspec= AIAB095945 Accessed January 2014.

Anon. (1951). "Architectural Education in the West, Montana State College." *Architectural Record*, 109(5): pp. 36–4, 36–6 and 36–12.

Carriel, M.T. (1911). *The Life of Jonathan Baldwin Turner.* Available online at: http://archive.org/stream/lifeofjonathanba011171mbp#page/n13/mode/2up Accessed January 2014.

Frye, D. (1993). "Linking Institutional Missions to University and College Archives Programs: The Land-Grant Model." *The American Archivist*, 56(1): 31–52.

Johnson, E.L. (1981). "Misconceptions about the Early Land-grant Colleges." *Journal of Higher Education*, 52(4): 331–351.

Milstein, E. (1951). "A Non-denominational Chapel at Montana State University," undergraduate thesis, Montana State University.

Stevens, G. (1998). *The Favored Circle: The Social Foundations of Architectural Distinction.* MIT Press.

4.9

LIVE

Between citizens and the state

Prue Chiles

> What are the real possibilities for you the architect in your position in
> society, not as hero who is going to save society, but as worker who is
> engaging practices that have the possibility of opening up new ways of
> doing things here and there ... that is linking with other people, not
> remaining outside of what else is going on, but being integrated into a
> general social and political process, ... and unfortunately, in so doing,
> having to make choices ...
>
> *(Harvey 1996)*

This quotation captures the highly political and contingent dimension of our
actions as architects. Talking to a well-known civic activist in Sheffield on how
he would describe the effect of our Live Projects on the City of Sheffield, he
explained: 'If there is anything good happening in Sheffield – Live Projects will
probably be behind it.' An exaggeration from an enthusiastic supporter perhaps,
but it made me think: 'What does this all add up to?'

Our 'Liveness' at Sheffield is not just about our fourteen years of Live Projects; it
is about an attitude we have built up and applied to our teaching, our research, our
consultancy, and our practice. There is an agency to most of our work that includes
people and is 'out and about' in the city region and further afield. Not just 'out
and about', but involved in and imbedded in communities. I think we can say that
all Live Projects are participatory and involve some form of co-production. Not all
our projects are enormously successful, for a number of reasons, or have a longevity
(discussed later), but we feel that they go some way to solving a challenge set before
us, as well as giving the city architectural ideas and helping people realize their own
ideas. We are often situated in an enabling or curatorial role, facilitating a dialogue
between citizens and the state.[1] So there is a political agenda, an understanding of
community and of neighbourhood. It is about rediscovering our own 'public man'.
They are necessarily political – they reflect the role of the architect and the question

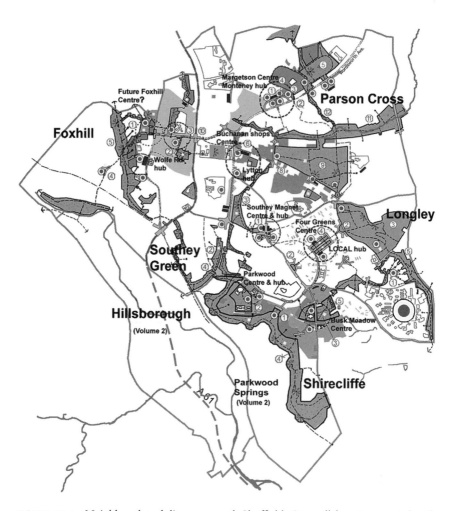

FIGURE 4.9.1 Neighbourhood diagram, north Sheffield. Our collaboration started with consultancy work in the Bureau–Design+Research (Bdr) to collaborate with the initial Framework Document for North Sheffield SOAR (Southey and Owlerton area regeneration). The report was the result of a three-year innovative process to construct a neighbourhood vision and framework document for all eight neighbourhoods working with local people throughout. Student Live Projects contributed to this process.

of what architecture education should be. Learning, after all, whether on the part of a professional or a student, is about 'a way of being in the social world, not a way of coming to know about it' (William F. Hanks in the Foreword to Lave and Wenger 1991).

Live Projects, like most things then, are about people and building relationships with people. Understanding processes of regeneration and renewal entirely depends on the people involved and the quality of the relationships built. 'We believe that

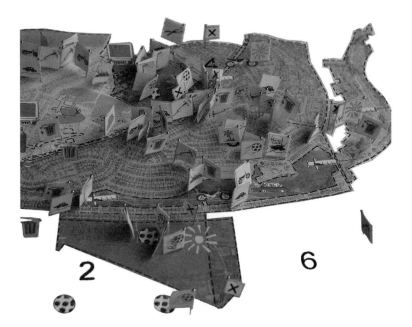

FIGURE 4.9.2 Participation mapping tools: Parson Cross Live Festival (2002) in David Blunkett's constituency. The first of five Live Projects that contributed to the framework document by working on a new neighbourhood high street and imagining better green and play space in one of the neighbourhoods.

high quality relationships lie at the heart of high quality processes' (Miranda Plowden, now Director of South Yorkshire Housing Association, pers. comm. March 2013). The nature of this reciprocal relationship and the skills sharing involved leads to an equal learning and teaching relationship between people. As students and mentors begin to understand complex systems and networks and stakeholder maps, that leads to the understanding of social organizations. Lave and Wenger (1991) re-thought the way we conceive learning. They placed the emphasis on the whole person and argued that we have ignored the quintessentially social character of learning and participating in communities of practice. This is at the heart of the potential success of Live Projects. We do not always have to be at the centre and can be in a supporting role. Most importantly, students are unthreatening and impartial, standing in the middle between the authorities and residents, and empowering residents through discussion and equal exchange to raise their aspirations and to become engaged and knowledgeable clients who understand the processes of design and development.

Getting involved in a civic life – and studying human behaviour by being there – allows us, according to Mauss, 'to perceive, measure and weigh up the various aesthetic moral and religious and economic motivations, the diverse material and demographic factors, the sum total of which are the basis of society and constitute

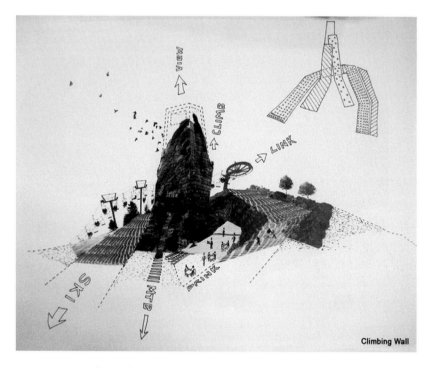

Climbing Wall

FIGURE 4.9.3   Parkwood Springs – what if? 2005 Live Project.

our common life, the conscious direction of which is the supreme art, politics, in the Socratic sense of the word' (Mauss 1990).

Our 'liveness' fits in with a recently renewed role for universities generally – the Civic University. Universities, particularly in a recession, need to take a bigger role and even leadership in the direction of the economy and renewal of the city. The Civic University is therefore high on the agenda again. Suddenly our work in the city is valued more and the impact is wider: Live Projects also constitute applied research, 'action' research with community partners, exploring wider societal themes.

We are concerned with the wider implications that our work at the School of Architecture has had on the region and what insights this may lead to, not only for the university (the academy) but also for the city and for the profession – for our future architects (see Chiles (forthcoming) on the work of the School of Architectures Bureau-Design + Research (Bdr) and the Live Projects). We believe we have been pioneers, as the century and the world changed, in developing our working practice into a democratic and participatory process of place-making, using creative engagement to understand and participate in the social and political structures in society. Participation demands many roles and ways of working, changing and facilitating, curating, listening, learning, teaching, and just getting stuck in. So we

Poplar Trees are effective at
screening noise, dust & smells
from the Landfill Site.

One of the largest Skateparks in the
country holding regional & national
events.

Landfill Site is active for
another 5 years.

Parkwood Springs could be an exciting new venue catering for the leisure and sporting interests of young people.

FIGURE 4.9.4 Parkwood Springs – a new skate village, Live Project 2012. Phoenix rising from the ashes.

have built up a repertoire of methods, tactics, and strategies that are useful, productive, and, at their best, highly skilled and innovative. One distinguishing factor of the projects is the breadth of task undertaken and we are expanding the field every year: from feasibility studies, website design, network diagrams, games, tools, and design processes tailor-made for organizations to architectural structures designed and built.

It is the effect Live Projects have had on the Sheffield region and the legacy in Yorkshire and the North that are perhaps most notable. We have contributed to regional and local strategies and to the gaining of funding for projects. Long-term projects have developed over the past fourteen years in, for example, the coal-fields region, the whole of Yorkshire, Accrington, Manchester, and Sheffield. Our most enduring collaboration in Sheffield, illustrated in Figure 4.9.4, shows how a long-term stake in a place can make an important contribution to shaping neighborhoods while working closely with the key agencies responsible for planning and development: local authorities, housing associations, and strategic regeneration organizations such as Yorkshire Forward. The projects usually have complex client bodies and a number of stages and demand a wide range of innovative participatory practices. Students every year have a growing body of work to build on and learn from. Primarily, though, the intention is always, as Doreen Massey states, 'to mediate between the wider strategy and the personal citizen's response' (Massey 2005).

Note

1 'Citizen' here is not discussed in its more politicized and contested way; rather, it is the simplest and most accurate way to describe where we are situated in the process.

References

Chiles, Prue (forthcoming). *Participation, Projects and Processes for Building Locally in a Global World*. Routledge.

Harvey, David (1996). 'Poverty and Greed in American Cities'. In *Reflections on Architectural Practices of the Nineties*, ed. W. Saunders. Princeton University Press, pp. 104–112.

Lave, Jean, and Wenger, Etienne (1991). *Situated Learning: Legitimate Peripheral Participation*. Cambridge University Press.

Wenger, Etienne (1998). *Communities of Practice: Learning, Meaning, and Identity*. Cambridge University Press.

Massey, D. (2005). *On Space*. Sage.

Mauss, Marcel (1990). *The Gift*. Routledge.

PART V
Closing thoughts

5.1

PEDAGOGY INTO PRACTICE OR PRACTICE INTO PEDAGOGY?

Two practitioners discuss

Daisy Froud and Alfred Zollinger

Editors' Note: This is a dialogue between two spatial practitioners working in two different regions who apply Live Project learning within architectural practice: Daisy Froud, principal of AOC Architecture and tutor at the Bartlett and the Cass Schools of Architecture, and Alfred Zollinger, principal of Matter Practice and Assistant Professor at Parsons The New School for Design. They had not met prior to writing this dialogue.

Initial considerations

What might be generated from two strangers coming together to write a chapter? How might the format of the chapter benefit from and exploit that? From the outset we both agree that, through Live Projects, we want to make practice more inquisitive and pedagogy more applied. This discussion models that way of working:

- Each made up to five statements about Live Projects, couched in the language of 'I think', 'I believe'.
- Each sent three photographs that perform a similar 'statement' function.
- Then each replied to the other.

The relatively clear structure may encourage the reader, as a third voice, to consider our perspective and then add his or her own.

Daisy's five statements/Alfred's comments

1. I believe that the opportunity to prototype a project, ideally at 1:1 scale, should almost always be taken, not least for the social and cultural implications it allows one to consider – the productive friction, the rub. At AOC we often organize events and activities at concept design stage with clients and potential users to test the dynamics of a project. It is a means to test theories of democracy, of engagement, of the politics of form, and to think about what theories and propositions start to emerge through the experiences and accumulated evidence.

AZ: What you are describing expands design into a much wider scope than the arrangement of objects and space within 'relational aesthetics'. The viewer/user is a participant in the design. The outcome is prototyped and developed in situ.

2. I believe Live Projects are important to help us (students and practitioners) learn and remember that architecture is always a compromised activity. Architecture is a social, cultural, and political process. Negotiations of all kinds must be positively engaged with while keeping one's eye on an outcome. And the fact that you inevitably lose some control over the outcome is a beautiful and joyous thing.

AZ: Very true – and it is annoying to think that most students only hear about this in a professional practice class. The 'letting go' moment you describe is very powerful and if practised in a controlled environment can be very empowering for students.

3. I do have some concerns about the implications of student-led Live Projects in terms of the expectations they raise among client groups. Given the kind of social interventions and pop-ups in fashion, students and schools might blunder in without appropriate social and political sensitivity – even if these are precisely the skills that Live Projects might help them acquire.

AZ: Failure is an option but I think, with a proper setup, this can be managed. Clients initially have lower expectations when working with students and support the work if they feel they are being heard. It helps if no money is exchanged for the students' services.

4. Discussing the efficacy of/theorising Live Projects is about the fundamentals of how we decide to produce space. The successful design and delivery of Live Project pedagogy requires considering – and taking a critical position on – the various power dynamics and decision-making processes through which the built environment is produced. Live Project work is not participatory fluff, or about getting a warm glow by being down with the 'community'. It is a way into thinking about space, power, and democracy.

AZ: It's about the production of space beyond theory; it's the design of the (design) process specific to its sociopolitical context.

5. I believe that practice stands to learn as much from academic Live Projects as education can learn from 'real-world' practice. I feel strongly that Live Projects – in the sense of trying out ideas in real space and time, working with those who will use or manage the spatial and formal outcome – have an important place in architectural practice. It's an opportunity to learn within the boundaries of a project, in a collaborative way, engaging with space and people and allowing these to challenge assumptions and 'hunches'. I think the most interesting work, and learning, emerges from that friction.

AZ: So true – teaching Live Projects has certainly made me rethink the way in which we practise and I imagine others would have a similar experience.

Daisy's images

1. Testing a project at concept design stage, using found objects, allows us to test assumptions about whether users like the look and feel of it, and also about how they might use space and form relationships with it and with each other. In Figure 5.1.1, I am discussing the challenges of 'free' use of future spaces and the level of control that should be the norm. The tent on a pulley is being used to explore how much people are really interested in altering the space themselves. The shower curtain circular space ended up being incredibly popular, and significantly influencing the final design, while the shed was extremely unpopular and completely left the picture!

AZ: This method of testing is one I could imagine undertaking in an academic setting without hesitation, but till now would have perhaps not considered in a professional one. You make a good case for testing more than material, construction, and formal aspects.

2. If a project is about the relationships it establishes, rather than a purely formal outcome, and the client too is curious and open-minded about how to get there, an intense testing period can allow everyone to learn together, with social

FIGURE 5.1.1 Testing event for The Lift (2007).

FIGURE 5.1.2 Testing workshop at Wellcome Collection (2013).

and spatial implications tightly intertwined. Testing ideas in real space is an opportunity not only to take tricky decisions in a collaborative way, but to productively engage with the politics of the project. In Figure 5.1.2 from a current project for an experimental gallery, we took up residency for a week in the host institution. In discussion with visitors, we learned about the ways in which people would like to interact with the collection, which informs not only the space's layout but also the mode of curation, the rituals of use, and how the room is staffed and managed.

3. Exploring the possibilities of the site and project in real space is an opportunity to get to know your clients and users in a very different way to that at a table-based meeting or traditional workshop. In Figure 5.1.3 we are working with the students at a school for children with autism to think about the new building's space and how it will relate to the existing building and garden. Perhaps some of the students are having more fun, running, jumping, and measuring, but we are gaining immeasurably from working with them, understanding how they perceive and use space.

FIGURE 5.1.3 Workshop with students, Spa School (2010).

Alfred's five statements/Daisy's comments

1. I think that architecture pedagogy should move away from the idea that projects start with a single author sitting in front of a white piece of paper (or canvas), as this is removed from architecture and space making. There is room for this kind of exercise, even though the most sophisticated modelling program still cannot make up for human experience and the fact is that most architecture is born out of resistance or friction.

DF: To me that is one of the joys of practice. In a positive sense, these things – the planning system, regulations, economic viability, a challenging site, a whimsical client – are the elements that shape a project. In theory the blank white sheet of paper is a 'free' enabling environment but that freedom can be paralysing, or generate more predictable 'creative' responses.

2. I believe teamwork takes on a completely different character in a Live Project because what is at stake is so much more immediate. Working out how to play different roles in varying circumstances prepares students not to be (or be able to be) in the lead all the time. How do you nurture an individual's design sensibilities and prepare her/him when practice mostly means working alongside others?

DF: Yes. Architecture is about your ability to communicate possibilities. It is more productive to see these acts of communication as acts of collaboration and co-creation.

3. It is critical to be able to 'toggle' between theoretical, abstract ideas which provide a reflective, contextual framework, and their real-time application or testing involving other people. Much progress has been made in the multiple ways architects practise, which in my mind is not yet reflected enough in schools. Too much time is spent in solving made-up problems.

DF: That is why I believe Live Projects need to be channelled into professional practice. Particularly in complex projects with multiple interested parties, it's important to keep a productive relationship between thinking and ideas, and practical activity (not that the worlds are so separate.)

4. I insist that students have the opportunity to test their ideas, to have to transform thought into something actual through an iterative process and incremental improvement. This moves them away from post rationalizing the first thing they imagine and into a process of finding opportunities. They lose the fear of having to compromise.

DF: There is always more than one 'option', and the first one, the 'purest' one, may not in the end prove the most effective.

5. I am convinced that students with Live Project experience demonstrate greater ability to adjust to changing conditions and are better able to interrogate a physical condition and know what they are drawing. This is evident in the confidence with which they make decisions while remaining open to changes. Having interfaced with clients/constituents and being able to anticipate feedback adds to their ability to remain agile and less defensive.

DF: One thing I have learned in ten years of practice is that architecture is as much about politics as it is about 'pure' design, sometimes to a frustrating degree. The ability to critically reflect upon the politics of the production of the built environment is invaluable.

Alfred's images

1. RISD thesis 1990, my first Live Project (Figure 5.1.4). *Fed up with the prevailing method of representation at the time, perspectives from highly controlled vantage points, I opted to present my project as an installation and performance at full scale.* It became an exercise of fitting, so to speak, both a physical intervention within the school's gallery space and myself into the profession (and the anxiety about it).

DF: I find that emergent process endlessly fascinating. There's a real opportunity there for post-occupancy analysis if the structure does get 'used'. And I would like to see more of that kind of analysis formalized within both education and practice.

2. Design Workshop Team/Splash House, 2011 (Figure 5.1.5). *This is what I think working on a team on a Life Project should look like.* All members assembled around a table talking with each other while simultaneously connected to the world. Surrounded by a white board, drawings, models, material samples, and

FIGURE 5.1.4   RISD thesis 1990, Alfred Zollinger's first Live Project.

books, they are sometimes deep in thought yet only need to look up to discuss issues, build consensus, and make decisions then and there.

3. Design Workshop/Splash House, 2011–2012 (Figure 5.1.6). *With the increasingly sophisticated means to render projects comes a false sense of being able to predict the exact outcome.* This set of images, which I think the students are very fond of, compares the final renderings of the pool pavilions and photographs of the built project.

DF: As critic and practitioner, I have the urge to chart the evolution when I see these before and after images, or rather the 'pure' vision vs. the delivered reality. One could apply a more formal structure, such as Actor Network Theory, or one can simply reflect on it informally.

FIGURE 5.1.5 Design Workshop Team/Splash House, 2011.

FIGURE 5.1.6 Design Workshop/Splash House, 2011–2012.

AFTERWORD

Mel Dodd

Architectural education appears to be entering a profound period of flux. Colossal fee rises and the diminishing prospects for employment are now shining an interrogatory light on traditional full-time pathways. In architectural practice, the boundaries of the discipline are expanding beyond building in inverse proportion to the shrinking role of the architect as lead consultant in large public projects.

And, as a consequence of these pressures, architectural education often seems to be retreating from the constraints and conditions of the real world, inhabiting a world of ideas. These divergent tendencies are not good for architecture students, or the building industry, or, indeed, society at large.

As a practitioner-academic, attempting to keep a foot in both territories, I have often reflected that architecture appears to be located within a problematic bind. The architectural designer is constrained by the necessities of regulation and control in the building industry – bound by professional, technical, economic and contractual agreements, and duties of care to clients and the public at large. Yet, at the same time, architecture has always been a social *art*, with (like venturous art and design practice) an ambition for engagement in the social and political: in resistance, enquiry, provocation, and intellectual risk.

The dilemma between these two essential, but potentially contradictory, characteristics is critical, because, most often, the former (prioritizing regulation and control) is more powerful and instrumental in the world than the latter – thus subsuming architecture's capacity for social and societal transformation. In consequence, city bureaucracies struggle to move beyond the status quo, rarely innovating or grappling with genuine innovations in processes or outcomes for the majority of their citizens.

On the other hand, architectural education, in an effort to re-balance these unequal forces, has tended to focus intensively (sometimes radically) on the latter – on ideas. The unfortunate outcome of this focus in the academy has been a gradual retreat from the constraints and conditions of the real world. Student architecture projects are often characterized by a rich narrative content and exquisite exploratory drawing and modelling, but (problematically) are also a critical distance from the reality of contemporary cities and their social and economic burdens, complexities, and constraints.

Architectural education, now more than ever, needs to re-situate itself at this nexus and offer young architects and practitioners the means to address these contradictory imperatives. But how can we operate at this problematic intersection and in the process avoid stagnating in the normative middle ground – dumbing down or diluting the radical potential of each essential characteristic in the process of trying to accommodate both?

Illustrated throughout this book are examples of possible alternatives for how to teach architecture through an engagement in different pedagogical frameworks of learning. These are alternatives that could be said to challenge the divergent tendencies of our discipline – either the retreat into ideas, or the normative technical resolution of construction – because they make the attempt to create a synthesis of both. These alternatives enshrine an outward-facing agenda that operates to radically address the schism between the academy and practice through an integrated and 'live' approach to projects, where the constraints, risks, and unknowns of reality are part of the process.

These projects help to show us that to be genuinely radical, architectural education needs to actively engage in the contradictory nature of architecture and spatial practices. We need – on occasion – to operate contentiously, even in conflict with the normative activities of the architect – to be subversive. But, at other times, we need to operate deeply and carefully within the constraints of constructability, legislation, and economic constraint – to be complicit.

Through an equal attention to both the subversive aspects (resistance, temporality) and the complicit aspects (fixity, regulation, reality) of practice we need to ask our students to engage in real intellectual risk. This is an intellectual engagement that does not inhabit an ivory tower, withdrawn from the difficult realities of the city, but rather engages with the everyday, and applies itself to the real world. We can draw some lessons from the past in our search for a pedagogy for practitioners. Traditionally art and design schools have always been places of applied and practice-based learning, many often historically established to serve the actual and practical needs of (then) contemporary society – the industrial revolution of the nineteenth century. Even in contemporary society they remain a place to establish and 'found' a future career by engaging in that career *during study itself*. Art and design practitioners have traditionally achieved this through the body of work that is produced at their institution. Designers cultivate an active engagement with community and industry through a variety of mechanisms: design projects for the real world, consultancy opportunities, placement, and work-integrated learning.

Architecture, too, can benefit from a more radical approach to education, and one that presents an alternative model, bridging the gaps between the lived and the built and preventing the formation of problematic schisms in the first place.

This is especially important if our disciplines seek to reclaim their roles as artists with social and political agency. Without application in practice – in the real world – the active potential of architecture (its agency) is untried and untested. And, in such scenarios, intellectual risk and experimentation, rather than being radically applied through actual practice, have the opposite effect – they retreat into an unfocused and esoteric speculation of the most abstract kind. Perhaps rather than a five-year withdrawal within the academy, we need to develop applied and situated learning as an integral part of the curriculum. At the most basic level, Live Projects for architecture and spatial practice are versions of project-based learning which have a real client and a real site – liaising with communities and agencies outside the university and often engaging with practical, professional, ethical, and sociological issues in a way that conventional (simulated) design studios can fail to. Moving beyond Live Projects alone, the potential for project-based consultancies for students can also be facilitated through organizational structures within the university-like project offices. And more radical still is the potential to unhinge study from its continuous or full-time institutional mode of study structure and to promote part-time pathways, periodic work and study options, and modular or short-course pathways.

None of these forms of learning are innovative in themselves, but when applied strategically to architectural training they are not only much less common and familiar to the discipline but also considered riskier for the way they might threaten conventional architectural education and the five-year degree. But perhaps it is time to threaten the norms of architectural education and accommodate instead a series of more dynamic, nimble, diverse (and economical) models, which could benefit students, universities, and industry, avoiding a 'one size fits all' approach. This would, after all, address another critical and neglected aspect of a rigidly professionalized pathway: the need to provide more diverse routes into alternative practices and careers. These might be careers which straddle and transgress the disciplinary boundaries between three-dimensional, interactive, organizational, technical, spatial, architectural, and city design, but which nevertheless provide essential creative thinking that contemporary cities and their communities need.

Picking up on this need for diversity, and casting an eye across the healthy gender balance of authors contained within this book, I have noticed that female voices are critical within architectural education with respect to accommodating other models of practice. This is because they emerge from, and speak about, what we might call more 'unofficial' personas of practice. These are roles that sit outside the mainstream narratives of how buildings get constructed. They can be, on the one hand, more mundane, prosaic, and practical – but, on the other hand, they can also be more complex, tangential, broad, and inclusive. The roles that women take on, rather than directing us down the middle path, often lead us instead to the defining edges of our discipline.

An acknowledgement and valuing of alternative and diverse models of pedagogy for architecture is critical because we also need to value alternative and diverse models of practice. And rather than see this diversity as the odd exception, we need to understand such models as critical inclusions that challenge, resist, and effect change of the status quo and entrenched values of mainstream architectural development.